2.

3.

This sketch shows the whole scene near
left hand corner opposite, and in particular throws up the
variety of roof line in the street. No 46, just off the sketch
is a mansion by comparison, with many cottages which foot
the same street, but its height is part of the variety
of the facade.

GUILDHALL

brick

brick

brick

brick reds brick

reds

32

34

36   38   40   42

44

MARKET STREET

, Market Street

variations in scale of buildings of similar style and
character of the street. This Georgian group is situated
south west of the principle facade of the Guildhall and
the urban quality of the street scene.

POOLE'S PRIDE REGAINED

1964-1974

by

JOHN HILLIER & MARTIN BLYTH

Poole Historical Trust

1996

This volume is published by the Poole Historical Trust, whose primary aims are the promotion of research, and the publication of works on the history and life of Poole and the surrounding area.

PREVIOUS PUBLICATIONS
The Pride of Poole
An Album of Old Poole
Mansions and Merchants of Poole & Dorset
Brownsea Islander
Poole and World War II
Portfolio of Old Poole
Ebb-Tide at Poole
History of the Town of Poole, 1839 (reprint)
Art in Poole & Dorset
Victorian Poole
Poole After World War II
D-Day Poole
The Spirit of Poole 1953-1963
Lifeboatmen Never Turn Back
Schools of Old Poole

Copyright © John Hillier and Martin Blyth 1996

First Published October 1996
ISBN 1 873535 30 9

Dust jacket and book designed by

Graham M Smith

has been responsible for the design of most of the volumes published by Poole Historical Trust. Born in Leeds in 1947, he came to Poole in 1972 as Assistant Curator of Museums, becoming Curator from 1977 until his retirement in 1993.

Andrew S Arnold

has worked on last six volumes published by Poole Historical Trust. Born in Portland in 1954, has worked in the Poole area as a graphic designer for the past twenty years and is currently a partner in Graphic Editions Partnership.

Production and film Graphic Editions Partnership
Printed in Great Britain by Bath Press Colourbooks, Glasgow

For John's wife
'SUSAN'
his confidante
and support
in those hectic days

ACKNOWLEDGEMENTS

The drawings of Poole Old Town on
the dust jacket and endpapers are by
John Mellings

Photographs and illustrations have also been supplied by

Mrs Edna Adams, page 108;

Arndale Property Trust Ltd, pages 34, 40, 44 (bottom), 45 (right);

Barclays Bank, pages 50, 52;

Martin Blyth, pages 23, 27, 94, 130, 135, 136, 163, 165, 166, 182, 184 (left), 185;

Ernest Bristowe, page 8;

D R Davis, page 95 (bottom);

F C Denley, King & Partners, page 174;

Hamworthy Engineering Ltd, page 104 (bottom);

Ralph Jessop, page 147 (top left);

Poole and Dorset Herald, page 10 (bottom);

Poole Arts Trust, page 159;

Poole Borough Council, pages 11, 12, 16, 19, 24, 26, 28, 35, 38 (bottom), 58, 59, 61, 65, 69, 72, 79, 90, 95 (top), 103, 105, 113, 114, 116 (main), 117, 119, 120, 137, 139, 140, 141, 146, 147 (top right), 148, 150, 151 (top), 154, 170, 173; and the official portraits of members and officers of the old Borough Council used throughout the text;

Poole General Hospital, page 92 (bottom);

Poole Museums Service, pages 10 (top right), 13, 17 (left), 41, 88, 99, 151 (bottom);

Suzanne Sieger, pages 91, 106, 107, 129;

Stanley Swain Collection, pages 18, 22 (main), 30 (top), 36, 37, 38 (top), 43, 44 (top), 62, 67, 74, 92 (top), 96, 98, 101, 111, 138, 147 (bottom), 153, 167, 169.

It has not been possible to ascertain the source of other illustrations used in the text.

Index compiled by Martin Blyth

CONTENTS

PREFACE

POOLE'S PRIDE REGAINED continues the story of *The Spirit of Poole 1953-1963* up to the dissolution of the old Borough and County of the Town of Poole in 1974. It covers what one pundit described as the time when Poole 'was dragged, kicking and screaming, out of the 19th century.'

He was probably right in that after the second world war, Poole's services and amenities were little different than they had been for decades. Its communications were poor; its street lighting was by gas; it had over 1,000 slum properties; its main shopping centre was stifled by two level crossings, and its employment opportunities depended greatly on its larger neighbour, Bournemouth.

The suggestion that there was widespread 'kicking and screaming' as these deficiencies - and many others - were steadily remedied, is, however, wide of the mark. Inevitably, there was strong opposition on some issues, from those who saw a particular project as a threat to old-established interests. Yet to readers of this book it will surely be apparent that the old Corporation, in the last decade of its existence, could not have achieved so much without the support of the great majority of the people of Poole. It would have been an impossible task if they had not wished for a better town - for themselves, and for future residents.

Thus it was a period in which the Council had both the confidence, and the resources, to put Poole into a condition that would also justify its citizens' desperate wish to remain an independent, free-standing town, not beholden to Bournemouth or to Dorset County Council. From the early 1950s Poole had campaigned at every opportunity to be given the right to manage its own affairs. In the years covered by this volume, it demonstrated on a broad front its ability to do so with considerable success. Fate favoured the borough with a number of Mayors of robust and colourful personality, who, even if they were political opponents of the ruling party, or personally opposed to some of the Council's initiatives, felt a general pride in the town and its achievements which they reflected in their many public engagements and speeches. The Council's forward-looking policies on housing, including the modernisation of older homes, as well as on sewage and refuse disposal, were matched by others that sought to improve the welfare of all members of the community. Better shopping and public library facilities, and the Arndale sports centre, were created. New Law Courts were opened, and a long-awaited public swimming bath was under construction. A purpose-built

Arts Centre was in view. Prospects for working people were improved, not only by the creation of industrial estates, but by a sense of vitality that encouraged major employers to move to Poole.

True, there were 'kickers and screamers,' not to mention that small company of persistent objectors whose wide-ranging zeal occasionally seemed to border on the fanatical. That is no more than one might expect, given the equally wide range of democratic freedoms, and rights of appeal, entailed in the process of local government. Yet one should not disparage the contribution of any of them to the eventual outcome. All sides in the debate knew that, after such momentous years, Poole would never again be quite the same place. It is therefore thanks to these various antagonists that one may assert that what was done carried a mandate from the majority of its citizens. As far as possible, it represented a collective vision of what the town should seek to be.

It was at a high point in its history that the old Corporation fell victim to the Government's reforms of 1974. It felt that its arguments for autonomy were still valid, and that it had deserved a better fate. It was, though, some consolation that Poole would still be represented by a separate, recognizable local government unit, the newly-created Poole District Council.

Derelict buildings in King Street.

COMPREHENSIVE DEVELOPMENT OLD POOLE

SLUM CLEARANCE AND REHOUSING

Poole Borough Council did not realise the magnitude of the problem when, in 1955, it resolved to clear Poole of all its slums in five years. A survey found that there were 987 slum properties in the town, 900 of which were in the Old Town. The very numbers would have made it a daunting task. When the Housing Minister could allocate only an extra 100 dwellings each year to rehouse the displaced tenants, the proposed time limit was impossible to achieve.

It was obvious that the clearance programme had to begin on the eastern side of High Street where the great majority of slum property was situated. This presented the Council with another impediment to any quick solution. Before rebuilding could take place, the narrow medieval streets and alleyways on to which the properties abutted would have to be replaced by a completely new road network. This root-and-branch solution meant that the Corporation would have to clear the whole area, demolishing not only the slum property, but properties in commercial use, and even properties scheduled as having architectural or historic interest.

There was considerable progress with widening of some roads and the construction of others, but progress in the redevelopment of the area was slow. By 1963, 55 slum clearance and compulsory purchase orders (out of the 79 finally required) were in various stages of implementation or Ministerial consideration; but only 231 families had been rehoused in the Old Town or in nearby Sterte.

Soon, however, a great increase in the rate of rehousing and the reconstruction of the eastern area of the Old Town was possible. In the following two years, for instance, 70 maisonettes, 64 one-bedroomed flats and 82 two-bed flats were completed. Other housing was under construction in the Old Town, including two further multi-storey blocks. With the help of 64 one-bedroom flats erected at Boyd Road, Branksome, 740 families from the slum areas were rehoused. By 1968, when Grenville Court, the last multi-storey block, was completed, all families wishing to remain in or return to the Old Town had been rehoused, and the Council could offer some tenancies in the block to those on its general waiting list.

This did not complete the Council's rehousing programme, for it had always been eager to maintain an appropriate population in the Old Town. It therefore built new property on the western side of High Street, notably on the old Poole Brewery's Malthouse site, which was once the grand 'Shrubbery' garden of Sir Peter Thompson's

Top left: There were nearly 80 public inquiries into clearance orders as redevelopment of the Old Town proceeded.
Top right: All change on the Old Town housing front: multi-storey flats tower over traditional terraced homes.
Below: The Malthouse site.

10

House. Here, the Council built 43 dwellings, most of which were let to applicants on the waiting list. Other living accommodation was also built by the Council in the Georgian precinct which brought the population of the Old Town up to the original target of 4,000 at a minimum.

THE NEW ROADS OF OLD POOLE

There had been little or no objection to proposals for redevelopment of the eastern area of the Old Town. These had gone ahead, despite some protest, before the plan for the whole area was approved.

It was very different with the redevelopment of the western side. The degree of local objection, primarily to the shopping proposals and the traffic way, meant that the agreement of the Ministry of Transport, as well as the Ministry of Housing and Local Government, was required. It had taken until 1963 to secure Ministerial approval of the plan.

Two new main roads were proposed. The first was to connect Lagland Street on the east to West Quay Road on the west. The second was a lateral road to take through

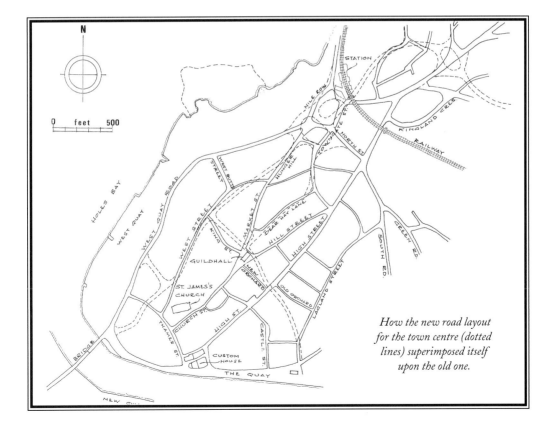

How the new road layout for the town centre (dotted lines) superimposed itself upon the old one.

Left: Looking from High Street towards New Orchard, which was widened and realigned to link the west and east sides of the Old Town.

Right: Creating an improved road link between the Quay and the West Street traffic way, together with demolition in the Castle Street area, provided a site for new offices and a multi-storey car park at Old Orchard.

Below: The southern extension (foreground) to Jolliffe House had to be demolished when an improved link was built between West Quay Road and West Street.

traffic from Poole Bridge to Longfleet. It would break through property to connect the north side of Poole Bridge to West Street. The latter road would be widened along its line to its terminus near Marston Road. The lateral road would then follow the line of Love Lane, finally turning to break through properties to follow the line of Market Street to a junction with West Quay Road, Dear Hay Lane, North Street and a realigned Sterte Road, where a large roundabout was proposed.

Building of the first road had already begun on the eastern side of High Street with the widening of Old Orchard, bringing the road from Lagland Street up to High Street. After that, it would cross High Street, follow the line of Bowling Green Alley, swing north round the Guildhall, and across the line of the lateral road. It was regrettable, but inevitable, that some High Street shops would be demolished.

The construction of the lateral traffic way (which adopted the name of West Street) and the new roundabout was a much more complex undertaking. Many properties had to be acquired. Having been accepted by the Ministry of Transport as a main road, the scheme attracted a 75% grant. This in turn required Dorset County Council to pay the rest of the cost from its overall Government grant, so more approvals were needed. The Corporation therefore decided to divide the work into four stages.

The first stage was to bring the new road up to West Street. It meant the purchase and demolition of considerable property, and a number of old houses, two of them over 200 years old. None of the properties, the Minister decided, was of great architectural or historic interest. This stage also required widening and reconstruction of the southern end of West Quay Road and the demolition of the southern addition of Jolliffe House. A reconstructed Bay Hog Lane would bring northbound traffic from the bridge back into the new traffic way. This allowed southbound traffic on the new road to divide between that turning left along the Quay, and that going over the bridge.

This complicated part of the new road was not completed until 1969. By this time, much of the preparatory work for the construction of Stage II had been done. This stage would take the road up to the newly constructed New Orchard road. It was relatively uncomplicated and was completed in 1971 at a cost of £46,000, nearly £20,000 cheaper than the short length and gyratory system at the Quay.

However, the construction of Stage III, designed to take the road up to the proposed Hunger Hill roundabout, was far from being uncomplicated. This section at first followed the line of the old West Street to its terminus at West Butts Street, then turned along the line of Love Lane, to cut across the back of the Roman Catholic Church in West Quay Road to the end of Market Street, where it was to join the new roundabout. This meant that the northern end of Market Street, from New Orchard to the point where it was closed, became a cul de sac, which was rechristened 'Market Close.'

Building the large Hunger Hill roundabout, and realignment and reconstruction of the roads to lead into it, was a very complicated operation. It impinged on the various buildings of the old Poole Brewery, the disused Hunger Hill Burial Ground, Garland's Almshouses and the densely built-up area round Nile Row.

Production at Poole Brewery ceased in 1905, despite having been a prosperous business under the management of Frederick Styring, a wealthy Yorkshire farmer. He had soon made his mark in Poole, becoming a leading member of the Council and buying Sir Peter Thompson's House. In 1852, he bought the small Poole Brewery, which he had expanded until it supplied 33 tied public houses. To enable the brewery to cope with the increased demand he built a new Malthouse in the garden of Sir Peter Thompson's House. The garden had originally run from the ha-ha in front of the house, in Market Street, all the way to Holes Bay. Then, to connect the divided operations of the brewery, a large underpass was built under Dear Hay Lane.

Mr Styring sold the brewery in 1880 and it later came into the ownership of Eldridge Pope of Dorchester, who closed it in 1905. However, most of the old buildings still existed in 1969 as well as the substantial underpass. The brewhouse, on the original site, had been sold and was partly occupied by Weston's Timber Supplies and Goddard's Shoes. A considerable part of a bus depot on the corner of North Street was taken down to make way for the roundabout.

The problems of the old brewery were not the only ones. At the entrance of the new West Street to the roundabout it was necessary to take off a portion of the disused burial ground of Hunger Hill. This work became a local cause célèbre when the contractors carelessly left a tomb uncovered. Some boys extracted a skull and bones which, the following morning, they proudly presented to their horrified teacher. They were later to tell a reporter that they had expected their teacher to be pleased with them!

Farther west it was found that the roundabout would require the demolition of Almshouses on the corner of West Quay Road and Hunger Hill. They were given to the town in 1814 for housing retired mariners. The Owen Carter Trust, which had long been responsible for them, was pleased to sell them to the Corporation. The sale proceeds, with a grant from the Government and a loan from the Corporation, allowed them to build 31 old persons' bungalows at Hamworthy. Even so, their demolition was considered an affront by some of the heirs to the memory of George Garland, the original donor.

On the northern side of the roundabout, a new extension of Sterte Road needed to be constructed which encompassed the forecourt of Poole station, the old railway cottage, and the densely built cottages of Nile Row, down which railway lines ran to the Quay.

Solving these difficulties and constructing the new roads and roundabout had to be done so as to allow traffic to keep moving. It was not until 1972, a year after the opening of Towngate Bridge, that the new road system was fully open to traffic.

TOWNGATE BRIDGE

The proposal in the Poole Plan to build a bridge to span the railway was not new. It had been proposed many times in the past. A poem written by Herbert Carter in 1926, referring to the frequent interruptions to all movement into or out of the town, complained: *Yet the town takes it all so calmly, – is there nothing to do or to say?*

It is possible the poem inspired yet another set of plans to build a bridge in 1927, then estimated to cost £77,000. These plans, like others before and after them, were sentenced to 'lay on the table'!

By the 1960s, both ends of the proposed bridge lay in heavily built up areas of the town, and its planning and construction presented formidable problems. The approaches to the southern end would have to contend with traffic using five other roads. It was thought this would require the construction of a large roundabout, which would need to encompass the whole of Nile Row and the southern end of Towngate Street. Realigning Sterte Road would take in the whole of Poole railway station forecourt and its cottages. What was more, supporting columns for the bridge would need to be sited in the area occupied by the station itself. Before this could be done, the station would have to be rebuilt elsewhere. At the northern end of the bridge, shops in High Street North would be demolished as well as property in Serpentine Lane.

It took until the beginning of 1969 to obtain possession of the 23 shops affected by the northern part of the bridge. By the end of that year, the site for the fly-over had been cleared. Much of the preparatory work, consisting of the diversion of mains and services, and the location of the ancillary roadworks, had been laid out.

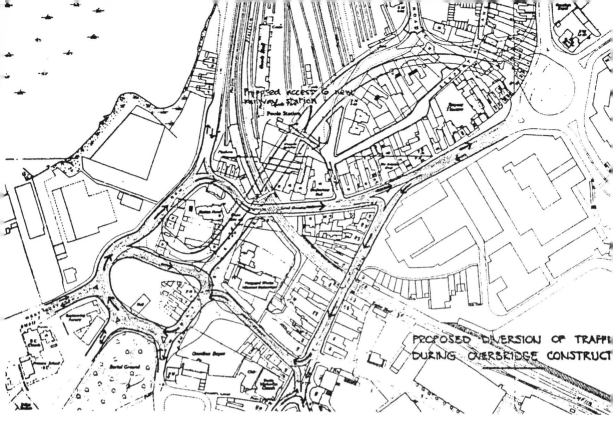

Within the image: PROPOSED ACCESS TO NEW RAILWAY STATION / Poole Station / PROPOSED DIVERSION OF TRAFFIC DURING OVERBRIDGE CONSTRUCT

Traffic diversions had to be carefully planned during the construction of Towngate Bridge.

In early 1971 the ramped approaches, across the end of Towngate Street on the southern end, and Serpentine Lane to the north, were built. This did nothing to soften the 'bombed out' appearance that part of Poole. The *Poole and Dorset Herald* wrote: 'The site is currently a hideous derelict piece of wasteland.' Perhaps the *Financial Times* was more understanding. It wrote: 'Poole is so busily changing itself that it is rather a mess at the moment.' By Spring 1971, the steel columns and beams had been erected and, in the following months, the white edged facing beams were attached. Suddenly, the form of the finished bridge was obvious.

September 30, 1971, was a long-awaited moment in Poole's history. Air Commodore John McIntyre, Chairman of the Highways Committee, invited the Mayor, Alderman Adrian Greenwood, to unveil the commemorative plaque and declare the bridge open.

In his speech the Mayor said that his parents had brought him to live in Poole. It was a beautiful town with a long and honourable history, but one that had allowed the 20th century to pass it by. 'It was an anonymous town,' he said: 'growing only slowly, and offering little in the way of facilities or work to its citizens. At last, the stranglehold the level crossings have had on our town for 100 years is going to be broken.' He went on: 'I feel to-day, a landmark in Poole's history, is one on which we can all shout from the rooftops because at last the stranglehold the level crossings have had on our town for 100 years is going to be broken...Poole will throw off the last remnants of the inferiority complex which has bedevilled us for so long.'

As the bridge was opened to traffic a motorcade of cars a quarter of a mile long streamed across Towngate Bridge, horns blaring in celebration.

Alderman Adrian Greenwood

Left: Towngate Bridge.

THE PRECINCT

The area proposed for the formation of the Georgian Precinct was in the south western corner of the Old Town. It lay between the proposed new traffic way on the west and High Street to the east, and between the Quay and the Guildhall in the other direction.

In 1963, when the Minister finally approved the Poole Plan, the area had an aura of total dereliction. On its perimeter there lay a working foundry, on its western side there was a mineral water works; and a thriving fork-lift truck factory lay immediately behind the houses of Market Street, with a wall and a boarded up secondary access from Market Street over the site of the old Dolphin House. Within the area itself, a range of old warehouses stretched along the eastern side of Thames Street. In Church Street was a builder's yard and, on the corner of New Street and Cinnamon Lane was

Main picture: Wessex Industries had an extensive site which extended into Market Street. It included the site of the old Dolphin Brewery.
Inset: The derelict ostler's yard in New Street.

the ruin of an ostler's store interspersed between the ruins of once prestigious houses on the corner of Levett's Lane was a struggling shop.

Most owners had long ago abandoned the houses to the squatters, tramps and petty criminals who had taken almost exclusive possession of the area. In 1963 the Rector of Poole described the area as notorious for drunken orgies in the streets, and unbridled vice in the many derelict houses, which reduced the area to *a Mecca for vagrants*. He did not exaggerate. The Yacht Inn at the corner of New Street and Market Street, one of the very few premises not occupied by trespassers, had become a dubious drinking dive.

With the passage of the Poole Plan the responsibility to convert this area into a Georgian Precinct became the duty of the Estates Committee of the Corporation. The officers therefore suggested that members of the Committee should acquaint themselves with it, and the problems that would inevitably arise. Early in 1963, a tour of the area was arranged for the members.

The officers had been dealing with slum properties for some years and might have become inured to the sight and smell of decay and human degradation. Members of the committee were perhaps influenced by the fact that so much of the work in the Old

High Street was never like this: patrons of the Arndale Centre on its opening day get used to shopping in covered "malls" inside a decorative, air-conditioned, artificially lit, pedestrian precinct.

Town to date had been classed as slum clearance, rather than conservation. Whatever the reason, the officers were completely unprepared for such a powerful reaction from the members, as they gathered in the road after their tour of inspection. They were unanimous in complete condemnation of the area. Each member maintained that it was unthinkable that it could be converted into a precinct. There and then, they unanimously resolved to recommend the Council to rescind the resolution to create a precinct! They even went so far as to declare to each other that no one would be allowed to persuade them otherwise.

'The Old Town is a complete shambles. Sanitary conditions are terrible. The whole place should be pulled down, excluding the Guildhall and a house or two near the Church,' exclaimed Councillor Monty Biles.

Councillor Ronald Hart said: 'Our visit to the Old Town has confirmed my long-held view that the old buildings should be swept away. The slum conditions are appalling, and no one will thank us in fifty years' time for preserving them.'

Councillor Leslie Miller said: 'It was with regret I found little to be saved in the Old Town. Years of neglect have made renovation impracticable.'

Councillor Geoffrey Adams said: 'Any action to preserve the Old Town should have been taken 50 years ago. I advise critics to take the same tour as we have done.'

As other members present spoke in a similar fashion, the officers were too shocked to argue. At every public inquiry into slum clearance and compulsory purchase involving demolition of property of historic or architectural interest, it had been stated that the precinct would be compensation for the loss. For the precinct itself to be lost at this stage, by a deliberate change of policy, would outrage almost every shade of public opinion. It would range from the most vociferous critic, who wanted everything ancient preserved, but had no idea how this could come about in practice, to the most sympathetic conservationist, who had so far gone along with the Council's line of reasoning.

No hope now for Old Town, the *Poole and Dorset Herald* declared, reporting that the committee was unofficially unanimous in condemning two-thirds of the properties originally scheduled to be preserved.

Between the meeting of the Committee and the following Council meeting there was considerable lobbying and arm-twisting. Some members, perhaps, recovered from the shock of what they had seen. Although certain councillors had to endure the taunts of those who remained firm, the Council reversed the decision - and honour had been preserved!

This, however, did not resolve the practical problems. The Borough Architect and Borough Engineer made a detailed study of all the properties in the area. They reported that all the properties in Cinnamon Lane and New Street (which included the mansion house of Samuel White, one of Poole's old merchants), were beyond any hope of saving; 49 properties could be redeemed - at a cost; and that 15 other buildings (including two partly demolished houses, together with other buildings, including workshops, warehouses, a builder's yard and a wall built across a vacant plot in Market Street) should be purchased and demolished.

Work began on a detailed study of each property to lead to the making of closing orders and compulsory purchase orders. Some owners were only too happy to be rid of their properties. After being condemned as slums, only the estimated value of the land on which they were built was paid, usually as little as £200. At quite an early stage the Corporation was able to offer a few properties on a long lease, subject to a detailed list of works of refurbishment and conversion being done.

The area, however, was still not in any condition to encourage new owners to undertake the costly works. The first few who volunteered found that Building Societies were unwilling to advance loans on such old and decrepit houses, and early progress was difficult.

In 1964, the Society for the Preservation of Ancient Buildings claimed the situation was one of *uncertainty, muddle, hopelessness and despair,* and warned that the area could deteriorate to the point where repairs were no longer economically possible. Even as late as 1965, Mr and Mrs Chaffey, both Councillors, were complaining of the lack of progress. 'Crumbling houses continue to harbour vice, and the Council's Special Precinct will be dragged into utter degradation. Boarded up in the afternoon, by midnight intruders have broken in, lit a fire and are drunkenly singing at the top of their voices,' they wrote.

In February that year, however, much to its own amazement, the Council carried a resolution that was to provide the means of preserving a historic street scene, whose continued existence was increasingly threatened by the passage of time. Members were faced with a report from the Chief Public Health Inspector that more properties were becoming unfit for habitation. Gasps of surprise could be heard in the Council chamber, when the Town Clerk announced that the vote was 14 to 13 in favour of an amendment to purchase properties needed to preserve the character of the precinct.

Alderman Ron Hart, chairman of the Estates Committee, who in 1963 called for decrepit buildings to be swept away, was one of the most astonished. 'I don't know where the money will come from,' he grumbled: but the decision was a sufficient mandate for the Borough Architect to bring forward a practical restoration scheme. Thus the point was accepted that the Society for the Preservation of Ancient Buildings had already made: that labelling an area as a precinct, in itself, did nothing to preserve it. Constructive proposals were also required.

One or two private individuals had faith in the eventual redemption of the area. Some properties near the church were refurbished by private enterprise. Mrs Eddie Frater redeemed an old shop in Thames Street and converted it into an antique shop. Arthur Coates and his nephew, Jurgens, took over the Garlands' old Mansion House in Thames Street, which had become a doss-house for itinerant lorry drivers. They worked for months to turn the decrepit premises into a restaurant, which opened at Christmas, 1964. In February of that year Poole House, a 17th century listed building in Thames Street, had been saved. Cracks appeared in the facade, which bulged outward into the street. Only a few hours before it was to be demolished as unsafe, the owners, Poole Foundry Ltd, decided to restore it. The house was encased in a corset of steel and timber while the front of the building was dismantled. Every brick and piece of stone was cleaned and replaced when the facade was rebuilt on deeper foundations.

Councillor Bert Chaffey

Old cast-iron gas lamp standards, refurbished and converted to electricity, became an feature of the street scene in residential parts of the Old Town.

In 1966 the Council agreed to renew the streets of the area, close some of them to traffic, and replace the street lighting with the original cast-iron gas standards, converted to electricity. It was not, however, until 1968 that real progress began to be obvious. Mrs Jane Hall took a lease of 10 and 12 Church Street and, with the help of her architect, Basil White, converted them into a single house. She then held an 'open day' there to demonstrate what could be done with old property.

By this time, the Corporation was offering loans to those willing to undertake to refurbish properties. Two or three members of its own architectural staff took up the challenge. The final seal of approval seemed to be given to the Corporation's efforts by Oscar Murton, the Member of Parliament for Poole. He moved into a house produced from the conversion of two old cottages in Church Street. They formed a pleasant, though rather eccentric, dwelling. Access from the lounge to the dining room involved going upstairs in one of the old cottages and down the stairs of the adjoining one!

Some of Poole's home-bred critics were not satisfied. The Rector, Canon Livermore, complained of the noise created by workers on night shift at Wessex Industries, the fork-lift truck manufacturers behind Market Street. 'So much for the much-publicised scheme to preserve Old Poole!' he wrote.

Jack Valentine's new house, built in 1974 next to West End House, incorporated bricks, tiles and other materials reclaimed from the demolition of ancient properties in the Old Town.

It was, perhaps, an indirect form of compliment to those who created the precinct that there were continuing demands for more to be done. The Corporation accepted that the Hants and Dorset Mineral Water works, immediately at the back of the precinct in West Quay Road, made dust and noise nuisance, and it eventually bought the premises. Criticism continued in 1973, when the precinct had finally been established. Canon Livermore, in the St James Parish Magazine, complained about the Crown public house in Market Street, saying he was convinced that 'the Precinct is the wrong place for such a din.' Peter Chase, the landlord, was irritated enough to reply. 'How the vicar is able to hear this, right at the other end of the street, is beyond me...and, in any case, I haven't heard any of the Crown's customers complain about the ding-donging of his bells!'

In fact, the landlord of the public house and his customers were soon partly relieved of the sound of ding-donging bells as Fred Price led his ringers out on strike, demanding '£1 a rope' for weddings, a dispute which lasted some time.

At least, few disagreed with the Corporation's own use of some of the cleared land in the precinct. A two storey block of flats for elderly persons was built at Cinnamon Lane, just off High Street, and they were much sought after. The site provided by the demolition of the old Greyhound Hotel and the closure of King Street was used for a block of 21 flats and two maisonettes. They were designed to complement the Guildhall and form a fitting boundary to the northern end of the precinct.

The award winning Guildhall Court flats.

This building, named Guildhall Court, won the Ministry of Housing's Gold Medal for Housing Design in 1970. The medal was presented to the Borough Architect, Geoffrey Hopkinson, and Michael Gooding, the design architect, by Peter Walker, Minister of Housing and Local Government, at a ceremony at the Architects' Hall in London. The building was also commended by the Civic Trust as 'illustrating admirably what time, hard work, careful designing, and good management can produce. It is an example of Conservation Area policy at work...'

Probably the biggest accolade for the precinct was bestowed in 1973. It was chosen by the Council of Europe as a pilot project to represent the United Kingdom in European Architectural Heritage Year, which took place in 1975. The Department of the Environment stated that the selection of Poole 'is a tribute to its being a forerunner in the development of a comprehensive approach to preservation.'

THE GUILDHALL AND MUSEUM

Of all the complaints about the formation of the historic precinct, the most legitimate were probably those about the condition of the old Guildhall. The complaints were encapsulated in a letter to the Press from a resident. 'It looks as if the Guildhall is about to fall down,' he wrote. 'The front facade is in a sorry state. Rusting wire netting clings to an equally rusting handrail. Stonework on the portico is cracked and crumbling. The hands are missing from the clock. The paint is flaking on the window frames. The once-elegant cupola has lost its weather vane. Why does there have to be a tin chimney up the side of the building, and the roof topped by a fire siren?'

Dorset County Council ended its tenancy of the Guildhall, which it used as an adjunct to its Technical School, in 1957. The slipper baths, which occupied the ground floor of the building, were no longer necessary, now slum dwellers had been rehoused and provided with their own bathrooms. The Council had already agreed to abandon the slipper baths and renovate the building. It would accommodate the Museum which, for 82 years, had been inadequately housed in South Road (previously Mount Street and now part of Lagland Street).

The work of refurbishing the Guildhall was completed in 1972 at a cost of £60,000. In June that year, Professor Barry Cunliffe, of Southampton University, formally opened the Guildhall Museum.

The Council had earlier appointed John Dockerill to be its first professional Curator. His ideas for displaying the Museum's exhibits were far different from the previous habit of cramming as many exhibits as possible into the small space available. He chose only a few artefacts, which he exhibited separately in newly-acquired display units.

Many of the older residents were fond of the old Museum, and its welter of exhibits, ranging from stuffed birds to antique pistols and locally found Roman coins. To them, the sense of exploration no longer existed among the carefully-noted, single exhibits and well-spaced display units. Many of the visitors, who had sometimes *totalled*

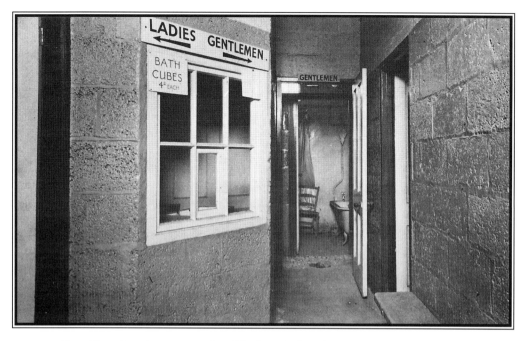

Above: The unimposing entrace to the public slipper baths which occupied the ground floor of the Guildhall prior to its refurbishment
Below: The interior of the Guildhall after renovation.

35,000 a year, were horrified at the transformation. One wrote: What on earth are Poole thinking about, in appointing a man in charge of our historical wealth at £3,500 a year, who suggests to Poole people that there is only rubbish in the old Museum, and that he intends only to show modern art instead?

The resident had his facts wrong regarding the new Curator's salary, and his intentions as to modern art, but he was not alone in his displeasure at the change!

THE FINAL PICTURE

For the most part, the many familiar landmarks of Old Poole, like most of its houses, had long ago ended their useful life and were unused and neglected. Yet they were often the only tangible evidence of much of Poole's history, and their disappearance in the rebuilding of the old town was felt as a loss by many of the older residents.

Even so, there were probably none who mourned the loss of the gigantic coal gantry on Gas Quay, or the aerial transporter from which dust blew over the eastern side of old Poole as it took coal to Pitwines gas plant alongside the railway to the north of the town. Nor did any regret the passing of the 'Fish Market' on the Quay. It had not been used by the fishermen for whom it was built since the day Mrs Kentish, the Mayoress, opened it in 1914.

The changing face of Poole Quay. The railway lines had disappeared but the Gasworks coal gantry was still in place.

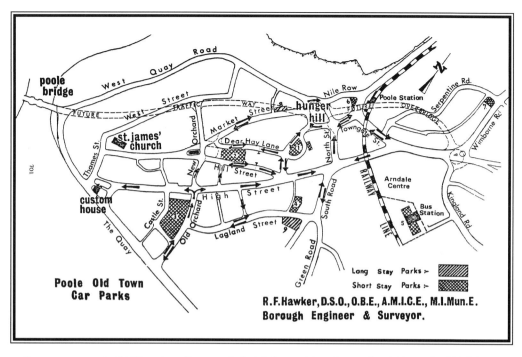

Improvements to the Old Town's traffic system included the provision of car parks within reach of High Street.

There was little sorrow at the demise of King Street, once so conveniently situated when the Corporation's business was concentrated in the Guildhall. The Poole Court of Record was established there, and the substantial Poole prison survived till 1967, converted to offices and a builders' yard by the Works Department. The original uses were long forgotten by the time the buildings in King Street were demolished and the road closed.

Few regretted the demolition of the last remaining building of the once extensive Lewen's Poole Foundry at the corner of Lagland Street and Green Road. Since the fire which in 1955 consumed the other remaining buildings, it stood as the last memorial of Poole's long history of brush making. It was an industry begun by Poole mariners, who whiled away long journeys from the West Indies by weaving packing fibre.

The disappearance of Rogers' Almshouses in West Street, and Garland's Almshouses at Hunger Hill, even though the buildings had long been empty, caused some regrets. There were more misgivings at the loss of many little lanes and alleyways in the Old Town and the demolition of Lagland Street School, where so many of its older people had been educated. To some members of the Salvation Army, the erection of new premises in Hill Street never fully compensated them for the loss of their 93-year-old citadel in Castle Street. Few were left who mourned the loss of the Unitarian Meeting House, whose members were once so influential in the life of Poole, or the Malthouse, a testimonial to the long history of brewing in Poole.

In fact, the main concerns of the public were centred round the increasing difficulties of communication. As part of the Corporation's concern to allow the rising tide of car ownership to move with relative freedom, it built multi-storey car parks in Hill Street and off southern High Street. It made High Street one-way; built rear service roads for the shops wherever this was possible; and gradually banned waiting in the narrow High Street. Eventually, it was necessary to charge a fee for parking, at first 1d [0.42p] an hour. When metrication was introduced, it was raised to 2p, to the disgust of many motorists who were unused to paying parking charges. One wrote to the newspaper warning, facetiously he thought, that 'they would soon be charging parking fees to make a profit'!

In 1973 the Arts Council commissioned two photographers, John Benton-Harris and Ian Berry, 'to reveal to the people of Poole how they and their environment are seen by two outside observers.' Their revelations took the form of an exhibition at the Guildhall Museum.

The photographers kept to their brief, for the most part photographing people of the Old Town. The comments of Ian Berry were appreciated, except that most people at that time did not think of Poole as a holiday resort. The town had lost most of its hotels and, although Rockley Sands Holiday Camp attracted 150,000 visitors a year, there was relatively little other holiday accommodation.

Ian Berry wrote: 'Poole, in mid-winter, not perhaps the ideal time to look at a coastal resort with only half the summer population remaining. However, the warmth of that half, coupled with the architectural variety of old and new town, made for a photographically stimulating situation, unexpected in a classically middle-class town.'

Council members felt rather pleased with their efforts during the last ten years to bring the town up-to-date and improve its amenities. They were far from appreciative of how John Benton-Harris saw Poole and its people.

He wrote: 'I don't consciously remember having a first impression, and find it hard to recall my last. Mainly it's because the place had no real identity for me. On the other hand, the people had. The transient people were out to enjoy themselves. Hamburgers, fish or anything with chips, washed down by delicious refreshing warm beer. So were the residents in their own peculiar fashion, slipping their 20-footers into the bay, lugging them about in cars, or on top of them, flashing their 20 HP Evinrudes and Mercurys, and generally prancing around like 20th century Lord Nelsons. But there's another type of person who can't afford to keep up with the Jones's, nor take holidays, but has to live there. His plight is the same the world over. In this case stuffed into overcrowded skyscraper apartment blocks in the midst of the redeveloped old town of Disneyland - oops, I mean Poole.'

It is said that in overhearing a conversation, one never hears anything good about oneself. Members of the Council were outraged by these comments. Alderman Fred Rowe expressed his disgust. 'As far as transient people are concerned, with their hamburgers, fish and chips and warm beer,' he exclaimed, 'I think he must have got off the train in Blackpool!'

Poole Camera Club was moved to respond. At the invitation of the Museum it staged another exhibition 'to reveal to the people of Poole how they and their environment' were seen by the town's "insiders".

Kingland Road, looking towards Longfleet from the old premises of Poole Grammar School.

COMPREHENSIVE REDEVELOPMENT LONGFLEET

ARNDALE

In early 1962 the Minister of Housing and Local Government issued his provisional list of modifications to Poole's Development Plan, following the Public Inquiry in 1960. They all referred to the plan prepared by consultants for additional shopping north of the railway in Longfleet. In his opinion the road layout and the distribution of new shopping frontages were unsatisfactory.

The Borough Engineer and the newly-appointed Borough Architect (Geoffrey Hopkinson) prepared a new plan providing for Kingland Road to be turned north to lead into a new, large roundabout near to the George Hotel, so sited that it would also be able to deal with traffic coming over the proposed railway bridge. The new line of Kingland Road also allowed more land to provide a traffic-free precinct of shops, stores and a supermarket, as well as a car park and a new bus station.

The Council appointed new consultants, Hillier, Parker, May and Rowden, to advise on the plan. The consultants enthusiastically supported the new proposals. Their report was submitted to a special meeting of the Council in January 1963, and, after a very stormy and acrimonious debate, the proposals were narrowly agreed.

As was written in *The Spirit of Poole 1953-1963*, it was thought that the argument over the future of trade in the Old Town was at last about to be settled, once and for all. All arguments and views had been fully aired and adjudicated upon by the minister. As the new plan embodied all his suggested modifications, early approval was anticipated.

The council therefore decided that the procedure to select a developer could begin so that negotiating final terms could go hand-in-hand with obtaining the Minister's formal agreement.

There was an overwhelming response to the Council's advertisement inviting developers to submit their names. The number of companies invited to submit outline development plans and preliminary offers was limited to 25. Of these, 20 submitted schemes, from which four were chosen to prepare detailed schemes and make firm offers of rent.

There were, however, signs that all opposition had not yet been stilled. *Traders' Secretary lashes town's administrators*, the *Poole and Dorset Herald* blazoned across its front page in October, 1963, *INCOMPETENCE CHARGE*. The traders' secretary was quoted as saying: 'There is no doubt in my mind, and the minds of many others, that the administration of this town is thoroughly bad. While some responsibility must be borne by those who are elected to serve in an honorary capacity, the major responsibility rests with the salaried officials...'

Traders' secretary lashes town's administrators

INCOMPETENCE CHARGE

'Bring in business experience'

SCATHING criticism of Poole Council and its salaried officials, whose administration was described as "thoroughly bad", came from Poole Chamber of Trade secretary Mr. David Hawkes at the chamber's annual meeting on Monday.

Speaking at the Port Mahon Hotel, he accused the corporation of incompetence, lack of co-ordination, and wasting time on official openings of buildings and estates.

Mr. Hawkes stressed that running a town the size of Poole was big business, and called for an experienced business administrator.

Mr. Gerald M. Hughes, advertisement manager of the Poole and Dorset Herald and associated newspapers, who was elected president, said the Chamber of Trade was not set up to tell people how to run their business, far from it, but properly used it could become a valuable asset.

"We need to combine our resources in order to reject and resist the pressures brought upon us by local authorities of today. And on the other hand there are times when we can even assist the local authority."

Mr. Hawkes' attack on Poole Council and its officers came midway through his annual report. After reviewing the town's traffic arrangements which were adversely affecting trade, he said:

"Wherever you look in the Old Town area, similar examples of incompetence and lack of co-ordination by the local authority are apparent.

"There is no doubt in my mind and the minds of many others that the administration of this town is thoroughly bad. While some responsibility must be borne by those who are elected to serve in an honorary capacity, the major responsibility lies with the salaried officials. Their conditions of employment are now so generous it must leave very little time to accomplish that which has to be done.

WASTED TIME

"Much of their time is wasted by official occasions to open new buildings and estates. Receiving official visitors takes more of their valuable time. Professionally, they are above reproach, as business managers they fall."

Running a town the size of Poole was big business. But it could only be run efficiently by employing an experienced business administrator, capable of co-ordinating the work of the various departments. He must be capable of accepting full responsibility and given the power to accept that responsibility.

On the council's revised proposals for shop development above the railway gates, he said they were not supported by the majority of traders. And although the proposals were passed by the council, it was obvious that had all council members been allowed to vote, then it would have been defeated. Those best qualified to reach a decision were barred from voting because of their declared interest.

NONSENSE

Since the re-development plan was first proposed three years ago events within the town in the intervening period had made nonsense of the arguments put forward by the planners aided and abetted by their business consultants.

In those three years private development of shops in High-street below the railway gates had already exceeded the amount of development envisaged above the railway gates. The lower end of the High-street, which in the view of the planners was obsolescent for shopping had made a remarkable recovery. It was attracting the smaller type of business, offering good quality merchandise at competitive prices.

In his president's address Mr. Hughes described their secretary's report as "stimulating, to say the least." They were fortunate to have a man of the calibre of Mr. Hawkes.

He hoped that during the coming year the chamber's executive would see wisdom in forming a "vigilance committee." From time to time traders were persuaded to part with money to doubtful causes and sources.

"I envisage that the work of a properly organised vigilance committee could effectively save many traders' purses. We must all project a confidence in the elected executive."

APOLOGY TO POOLE COUNCIL OFFICERS

IN our issue of October 30, 1963, we published a report criticising the salaried officials of the Poole Town Council in a speech by Mr. David Hawkes to the annual meeting of the Poole Chamber of Trade.

We wish to make it clear that charges of incompetence, bad administration and wasting time were in our opinion completely untrue. We in no way support Mr. Hawkes' criticisms of the salaried officers of the Corporation and apologise to them for the adverse publicity given to the charges implied in Mr. Hawkes' speech.

We have agreed to indemnify the officers for the expenses which they have incurred in vindicating their reputations. We would also like to make public that to mark the sincerity of our apology we also offered to pay to the chief officers and deputies substantial damages, which they have waived.

Top: The newspaper article that provoked a libel writ from officers of the Borough Council.
Bottom: The libel action was settled by a public apology and the payment of costs. The offer of substantial damages was waived.

These criticisms mostly related to other aspects of the Corporation's work: but at a delicate stage in the development, it was important that the members' resolve to complete it should not be undermined by the advice of its chief officers being weakened.

The Town Clerk and Chief Officers, joined by the Deputy Town Clerk and Borough Treasurer, therefore served a writ on the newspaper alleging that they had been libelled. The pleadings in the case continued until the following May when the newspaper offered the officers a sum in damages and a public retraction. The officers declined the offer of damages but otherwise accepted the offer.

Meanwhile, the four chosen development companies had submitted detailed plans and artists' impressions. All four proposals were impressive and would have provided the town with a fine new shopping precinct, as well as a rent in excess of the consultants' estimate.

Before making a final recommendation, the consultants advised that they and some of the Chief Officers should meet the boards of the companies involved. The object would be to assess their commitment to the scheme and the officers' confidence that they could work with them.

Two of the companies were subsidiaries of the two largest property companies in the country, MEP and Land Securities. It became clear that all four companies had taken the proposal most seriously, and were completely committed to carrying out their submitted schemes. This was clearly demonstrated by Lord Samuels, the Chairman of Land Securities. He demanded that the members of his board return from Ascot races to attend the meeting. Still in their Ascot morning coats they made an impressive group!

Something else made this meeting linger in the memory of the Town Clerk. When it went on longer than anticipated, he had to excuse himself to make a dash for a train to attend a meeting in Poole that evening. Once outside the offices in Park Lane, he was lucky enough to see three or four taxis travelling down the road. He hailed the first cab, whose driver slammed on his brakes. The second cab, having no chance to swerve, tried vainly to stop before colliding with the first, and the third cab ran into the back of the second one. Each driver quickly got out and blamed the other for the collision. While they bounced their cabs on their springs to try to disentangle their bumpers, another cab came down the road and picked up the fare. The Town Clerk always felt a residual guilt for the collisions.

However, despite these impressive meetings, nothing transpired to alter the view that the detailed offers of PIC (Property Investment Consolidation) Ltd and Arndale Property Trust Ltd were the better ones, as well as offering the largest rental.

PIC's proposal, accompanied by a large-scale, most impressive model, was to provide an open-air pedestrian precinct with shops arranged round a large, central piazza, with fountains and trees, and with canopies, twelve feet wide, along and between the shopping frontages. The company offered an annual rental of £80,153 for a 99-year lease. Arndale offered what was then a unique, under-cover, heated, air-conditioned precinct with a ten-pin bowling centre and a dance hall built above the shops. This proposal gave full protection to shoppers as well as giving height to the building, which was considered a considerable architectural merit for the centre of the town, as well as providing for some social activity. Details of both schemes were submitted to the Council with the recommendation to accept the Arndale bid, even though its offer of a ground rent of £76,500 was less than that of PIC.

Not all members agreed. There was no precedent for Arndale's proposal of an enclosed shopping precinct. The only existing development approximating to it which Arndale could cite was in Toronto, Canada. The directors of Arndale offered to fly the Town Clerk and Borough Architect to Toronto to see such a development for

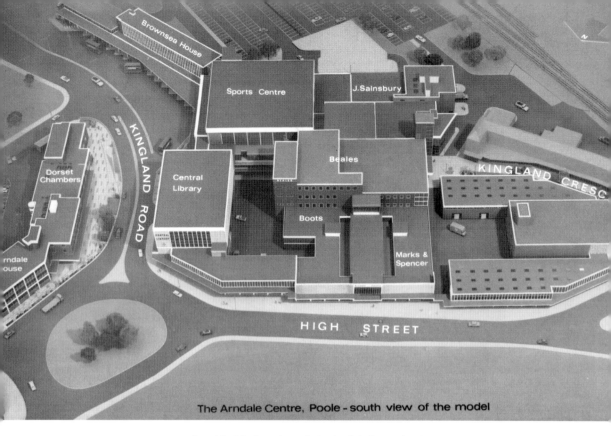

The Arndale Centre, Poole - south view of the model

A model of the first phase of the Arndale Centre development.

themselves, but the officers, still conscious of the traumas of a libel suit, declined the temptation! Some members claimed that the concept was 'just a gimmick,' and that the Council should opt for the safer, more conventional, scheme of PIC, especially as the rent was greater. After some debate, with 22 out of a total of 40 members voting in favour of Arndale, the Redevelopment Committee's recommendation was agreed.

The Borough Treasurer estimated that, at the rent offered, the Council should show an annual surplus of £47,270 which would possibly increase at review periods, amounting to a surplus of over £80,000 after 60 years, when the Council's borrowings would have been repaid. It would, too, give the Council an increased rateable value of £125,000.

Meanwhile, in February 1964, the Minister issued the final decision on the original Poole Plan. The long delay had already upset the timing of the scheme. Even so, there was a reasonable hope that the Corporation would have all necessary consents by the time work was ready to commence.

These hopes faded when seven objections to the new plan were made and a public inquiry could not be held until February 1965. There was only one new genuine objection: from a chemist on the corner of Kingland Road and High Street whose site was affected by the proposal to turn Kingland Road further to the north.

The minister agreed it was not possible to omit this site. The south-east side of High Street North, he said, suffered from an obsolete road layout. The backs of the buildings in it were exposed, and the indifferent shopping frontages to High Street were both inconvenient and wasteful. It was therefore necessary to have an overall plan and for Kingland Road to be realigned. More precious time had been lost by the time his decision to approve the plan was announced in September 1965.

Ministerial approval was also necessary for various steps needed to implement this decision. They included a compulsory purchase order for 38 acres of land and buildings; formal sanction for the Corporation to borrow the necessary money; a Certificate of Appropriation for Ladies' Walking Field; and an order to extinguish public rights of way over Longfleet Place, Serpentine Lane, and parts of Kingland Road and Kingland Crescent.

Though all these matters had been gone into at earlier inquiries, a few objectors took advantage of the chance to raise them again. Their lack of genuine grievance was demonstrated by the fact that there were never more than seven objections. Most were withdrawn at the start of the public inquiry. Some objectors did not even bother to attend.

The order that created the greatest public uproar was for compulsory purchase of the land required. The objectors gained encouragement from an article in the *Sunday Times* in September 1965. It bewailed the sight of empty shops in Bristol, Derby and Burton on Trent as well as in Leek, Manchester and Middlesborough. 'In these towns,

Properties on the eastern side of High Street, north of the railway line, were demolished to make way for the Arndale Centre, the realignment of Kingland Road, and an enlarged roundabout at the George Hotel.

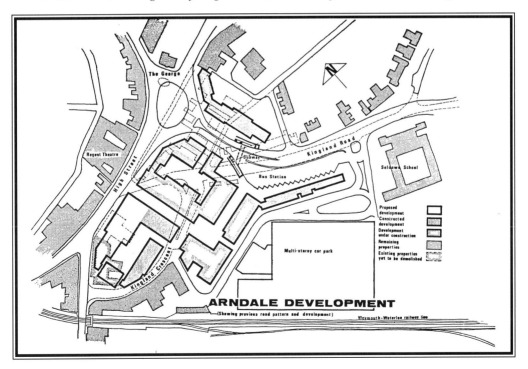

Top: Looking towards Longfleet from Topp's Corner, the junction of High Street and Towngate Street. The former Dolphin Hotel is on the left. Much of this area is now covered by Falkland Square.
Below: Another view of Topp's Corner. The Ansty Arms public house stood on a triangular site on the right of the picture. Beyond it, most of the buildings on the eastern side of High Street, between the George roundabout at the level crossing, were demolished to make way for the Arndale development.

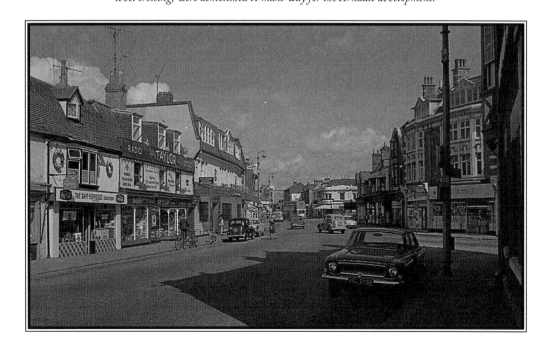

and in a good few towns besides, what you see is a sad cluster of empty shops in buildings which have been put up and finished for at least a year...These empty shops are the rashes of a disease which, for the past 18 months to two years, has been gradually spreading...all over England as the market swings from a straight seller's market to a buyers'...After 11 months of credit squeeze...developers' problems are there for all to see...'

Opponents were given new heart to continue their implacable opposition. The public were exhorted to *stop this reckless administration of Poole property,* to *get rid of the planners before they bankrupt the borough,* and to throw out any councillor who continued to support the Ladies' Walking Field 'flutter.'

If the aim of the objectors was to delay the scheme, they succeeded: but it was their only success. Despite opposition every step of the way, the Compulsory Purchase Order was approved. The Minister gave his sanction to borrowing the necessary money, approved the extinguishment of rights of way, and gave his Certificate of Appropriation of Ladies' Walking Field in March, 1966.

A few months later, the loyal patrons of Lill's Cafe, which stood in Kingland Road opposite the junction with Kingland Crescent, heard that their rendezvous would soon be no more. Neither the Council nor the developers had any suitable alternative accommodation for a business based on fourpenny cups of tea and one-shilling rounds of sandwiches. The proprietor, Mrs Lily Pearce, was offered compensation for its closure; but for generations of customers, including many drivers and conductors from

A later stage in preparing the Ladies' Walking Field site for the Arndale development.

Above: As more buildings adjoining the Longfleet end of High Street were cleared, the new line of Kingland Road began to emerge.
Below: Hill Street multi-storey car park.

Alderman Arthur Lloyd-Allen

the Hants and Dorset bus terminus in Kingland Crescent, the loss was irreplaceable.

What might have been a triumphant and whole-hearted approval for the re-establishment of Poole's commercial centre proved to be a long, wearisome battle of attrition. Alderman Lloyd-Allen and his Redevelopment Committee stuck determinedly to their task. When he reported receipt of the final approval, he could not resist remarking to the Council that 'the delay has cost the Corporation and the rest of the population thousands of pounds in interest charges and loss of rent - as well as the deferment of facilities and amenities which we have worked so hard to provide.'

He ruefully ended: 'I am all in favour of sustaining all our domestic freedoms but, unfortunately, even freedom can lead to excess, and a tiny minority can, by using them, oppress and delay the will of the majority for long periods.'

In making this statement, he undoubtedly felt that his last ordeal was over, and that the Committee had finally won the long battle: but relief was short lived. A day or so later, the Council was served with a notice informing it that one of the two objectors to the appropriation of Ladies' Walking Field had been given leave, by the High Court, to bring an action challenging the validity of the minister's Certificate of Appropriation!

At last, an objector had put himself in a position where he had something to lose. The Corporation gave notice of their intention to oppose the case and counterclaimed for their costs and for the payment of substantial damages that would be caused by further delay to the project. The Corporation also applied for expedited hearing of the case, but was advised that a hearing was unlikely until the following Spring.

By this time, the Council and Arndale were already struggling with yet a further problem. In July 1965, the Government issued an edict, popularly called 'the Callaghan Clamp', to restrict all building work. In December, Parliament passed the Building Control Act, 1966, which forbade all building work costing over £50,000 without the licence of the Ministry of Public Building and Works.

While the Corporation and Arndale were struggling to get clearance from the ministry, the Corporation received some good news and some very bad news. The good news was that the plaintiff in the High Court case had withdrawn his action. The very bad news came in a letter from Mr S H Chippendale, managing director of Arndale. His parent board, he wrote, had reviewed their arrangements with the Corporation. It was 'necessary to ask you to look into the possibility of re-arranging the basic terms.'

Sainsbury's supermarket in the Arndale Centre was the first to forsake a traditional High Street location. When it opened, Lord Sainsbury, the company chairman, came to welcome the first shoppers personally. Any fears he made have had about how the new store would trade were soon answered. It became one of the busiest Sainsbury's of its size anywhere in the country.

Inflation, he said, had increased building and finance costs to such an extent that the project was no longer viable. The only way to make it so again was to omit the 'unproductive' parts of the development. This meant the omission of the proposed ten-pin bowling centre and dance hall.

The Town Clerk and Alderman Lloyd-Allen rushed to London to discuss this dramatic turn of events with the consultants. Mr Chippendale was summoned to a meeting the following day at the offices of the consultants, at which Alderman Lloyd-Allen, the Town Clerk and Bob Cass, the Deputy Town Clerk, were present. There was no disguising that the development had been delayed beyond anything which could have been contemplated when terms were tentatively agreed. Nor could it be argued that there had been no inflation during the period, or that building costs had not risen by at least ten per cent, and the cost of borrowing by at least one per cent.

Sainsbury's supermarket helped to introduce the concept of family shopping to the Arndale Centre.

Alderman Mrs Elsie Hickinson. *Leonard Shaw, Borough Librarian.*

The Town Clerk and his deputy had been in regular contact with the officers of Arndale for some time, while units in the centre were being pre-let, and Sainsbury's were being persuaded to open their first shop which did not face a main shopping street. The officers already knew it was probably impossible to get a ten-pin bowl for the new centre. The franchise owners refused to consider any further ones in Poole or Bournemouth. The officers also knew of the fruitless efforts of Arndale's agents to pre-let the dance hall.

The Corporation's small delegation decided that there was little purpose in denying facts that were demonstrably true. It was thought essential to maintain a rental income of £76,500, retain the proposed height of the new centre, and prevent further delay in building it. These basic requirements were agreed, subject to the Corporation taking over the 25,000 square ft of the building on the second and third floor, designed for use as a dance hall. This could be used to provide a new central library. It was hoped the Council would agree to provide a sports centre in the area first proposed for a ten-pin bowl. Arndale agreed to contribute £60,000, half the estimated cost of building a 'one-court' sports centre. The Corporation agreed that Arndale would retain the ownership of two blocks of flats in Mount Pleasant Road, which the company had bought to rehouse displaced tenants, and that the flats would not be transferred to the Corporation, as previously determined.

These inchoate agreements had to be given substance and be approved by the Council. The proposal for the central library was fairly straightforward. Alderman Mrs Elsie Hickinson, Chairman of the Libraries Committee, and Leonard Shaw, the

Borough Librarian, were delighted with the prospect of a new central library, and considered the site was an improvement over the previously agreed one in the Civic Centre. The Council would pay the estimated cost of £250,000 from its capital receipts, and the Ministry agreed, subject to a lift being provided to the lending library.

The proposed Sports Centre was a more difficult proposition. Some Councillors could see only a prospect of having to pay permanent subsidies. 'If it was considered that four squash courts were needed in the borough,' one commented, 'why had not any been provided by private enterprise?'

There were the usual opponents to anything to do with the centre, with arguments as to the likely failure of the proposals and the wrong siting, especially of the new library. There was more serious opposition from Councillor Geoffrey Adams. Formerly Chairman of the Redevelopment Committee, he was the member who first put the case for the centre to be built. He complained that the proposed amendment of the 'much vaunted shopping scheme' was one reason 'why local government has fallen into disrepute.' The major factor in the choice of Arndale had been that it offered the greatest range of uses, including entertainment facilities, covered and illuminated shopping facilities. It had repeatedly been stated that the Arndale scheme would include a dance hall and bowling centre. 'I and the citizens of Poole have been the victims of broken promises,' he claimed.

In May, Alderman Lloyd-Allen had the task of persuading the Council to accept the new arrangements. The most the Council would agree to was to contribute a sum toward the proposed sports centre and to meet its running losses for two years. Substantial responsibility for it would have to lie with another body. On this basis, the Council agreed to the new contract with Arndale.

Kingland Road, looking towards High Street, before the Arndale Centre development began.

The new line of Kingland Road begins to take shape, as cottages opposite Ladies' Walking Field face an uncertain future.

Walk-in shops, with no doors, pavements or busy roads to negotiate, were a novelty for customers at the Arndale Centre in 1969.

In November 1966, Arndale received a building licence from the Ministry of Works. The Corporation arranged to provide a sufficient area of the site for work to commence on February 1, 1967, some two and a half years later than first planned.

In 1967 the roads and sewers contract was completed by the Corporation at a cost of £135,000, and the new George roundabout was partially opened. A contract was signed for the first part of a multi-storey park for 388 cars to be built at the rear of the development, at a cost of £120,000. With the provision of a further 285 spaces for surface car parking, it would give a total of 798 parking spaces by the time the centre opened.

The total net cost to the Corporation was estimated by the Borough Treasurer at £844,400, which included the cost of the land to be taken for car parking. This would give the Corporation a net annual profit of £37,800 in the early years and, though rent reviews were provided for, a substantial increase in rent could not be expected before the year 2012.

In 1967, even as the centre was being built, the Corporation was approached with an offer for its lease which would yield a profit of at least £500,000 after the extinguishment of debt. It was not interested to selling the lease, but the offer came as a welcome boost to its confidence in the eventual success of the venture.

An aerial view of the Arndale Centre. Kingland Crescent, which was transformed from a bus terminus to a pedestrian shopping precinct, is on the right of the picture, adjacent to the railway line.

Public seats were not plentiful in High Street, but in the Arndale Centre there was plenty of room for shoppers to relax and chat.

The Barclays House site, overlooking the George roundabout. The old Poole Grammar School premises in Kingland Road are at the top right of the picture.

Another view of the Barclays House site.

BARCLAYS BANK DCO

Many properties were acquired by Poole Borough Council to clear the large area needed to build Towngate Bridge. The process to acquire the land began in 1966, after the Ministry of Transport promised to approve the start of work on the bridge in 1969/70.

For the approaches to a greatly extended George roundabout, properties in the area of High Street, Serpentine Lane and Serpentine Road had to be bought. The line of the bridge, being roughly south-north, cut across many existing boundaries. As a consequence, the Corporation had to buy a considerable area of the land to the west which was not required for the bridge.

That left an 'island' site of about three acres between the west of the bridge and four houses on the west side of Serpentine Road, which backed on to the Corporation's central depot and its stadium in Wimborne Road. There also remained on this site a number of houses, interspersed by an electrical equipment factory, a wholesale fruiterer and other property used for storage. The Corporation felt the area, which would be dominated by a bridge which rose to a height of 27 feet, needed comprehensive development. Part of it had already been proposed for commercial use in the 1960 Poole

Plan. In 1967, the Corporation unsuccessfully applied to the government to agree to its use for offices under its Town Centre redevelopment scheme.

In 1969, when the Corporation was asked by Barclays Bank DCO [Dominion, Colonial and Overseas] whether it would welcome part of the bank's operations being transferred to Poole, it had no hesitation in replying that it would welcome such a move.

When a representative of the bank met the Town Clerk in March, 1969, he outlined its requirement for a building to provide about 350,000 square feet of office space and car parking for 1,600. He had already visited most of the 16 towns selected by his board as possible locations.

The officers took him to see the site to the west of the bridge. The Arndale Centre was nearing completion. Work was also in progress to enlarge the George roundabout and clear properties for the bridge. The area was more like a confused builder's yard than a prestigious site for a bank. The officers explained what was going on and offered apologies for the apparent turmoil. They were encouraged when their visitor brushed them aside. He said it was a change, from hearing of the future plans of so many other towns, to find one that was actually putting them into practice.

Soon after, it was confirmed that from a final short-list of four towns, including Worthing and Cheltenham, Poole was the one with which the bank chose to negotiate.

The site for new offices envisaged by the council was merely the island site of some three and a half acres, lying to the west of the proposed bridge, and bounded by the enlarged George roundabout and Serpentine Road. However, the water table of the land precluded the construction of an underground car park. To be able to erect a multi-storey car park for 1,600 cars, it would be necessary to acquire the site of four properties on the north side of Serpentine Road, which would bring its boundary up to the Corporation depot and Stadium.

It was this extension of the site which became a cause célèbre in the town. The owners of property on the north side of Serpentine Road were horrified to learn that their homes were included in a compulsory purchase order. Mrs Joan Clements, at 21 Serpentine Road, would have her life seriously upset. Her husband was often on stand-by for duty at nearby Poole Hospital, and her children attended local schools. Mrs Sheppard, who had lived at 23 Serpentine Road for 25 years with her two sisters, one of whom was deaf and the other blind, was also extremely disturbed at the prospect of losing her house, as was Mrs Winifred Giles at 59 Wimborne Road, a large house with a flank frontage to Serpentine Road.

The only alternative to taking these houses was to acquire land from Poole railway sidings. It seemed an unlikely prospect, but British Rail was eventually persuaded to sell. This would allow the car park to be built without requiring the site of any of the houses, but it would still infringe the daylight code at 21 Serpentine Road. Though the Corporation was able to assure other owners that their property would be deleted from the compulsory purchase order, it was felt, much to the anguish of Mrs Clements, that the order on her house must be retained.

The architects' plan showed the new bank building to be erected on the island site with a car park for 1,600 cars in its new situation. The building had a central core, 145 ft high, surrounded by three hexagonal wings, each 138ft high, and provided 436,000 square ft of office space, with a basement. It was anticipated that building work could begin in 1972, with occupation of the offices in mid-1974. Town planning approval was given by the borough as well as the county council by mid-1970, but the planning application and compulsory purchase order were 'called in' for consideration by the Ministry. It was not until the end of February 1971 that a public inquiry was held. By this time the bank and the Corporation had bought much of the land required by agreement. The electrical equipment factory had relocated itself into a more appropriate area, as had the wholesale fruit warehouse, and the other warehouses; and ten of the twelve residential properties involved had been acquired by the bank.

At the public inquiry, Mrs Clements was the only property owner who had a substantive objection, but there were seven other objectors, including the Joint Committee of Poole Residents and Ratepayers, Poole Labour Party, two nearby residents, and two of the town's inveterate protesters. Mrs Clements wanted the car park built farther from her house, as it would cause serious hardship in the loss of amenities and light. Others claimed that the importation of 800 staff to the town would seriously strain its schools, health services, social facilities and public amenities, and cause serious traffic congestion. Poole Labour Party's representative suggested another site for the bank in the northern part of the town.

The Town Clerk presented the council's case. He outlined many benefits that would accrue from the establishment of the bank in the town, and the efforts to site the car park farther away from Mrs Clements' house. The council had even offered not to enforce the compulsory purchase order, and to purchase her house, if she later changed her mind, at a price which would not be reduced by the presence of the car park.. The council had no other alternative but to ask for the compulsory purchase order to be confirmed.

On behalf of Barclays Bank DCO it was said that the bank considered the merits of many other towns. Poole was the only town which fully met its requirements. Its proposal had been welcomed by the Department of Employment and the Youth Employment Bureau as well as the Corporation and the county council. The bank had even established a pilot scheme in offices rented at Frizzell House, County Gates, which some 100 staff had operated very successfully. Within two years, it expected to employ about 2,000 staff in the new building, of whom some 1,000 to 1,200 would be recruited locally.

The Minister granted planning permission and approved the compulsory purchase order in August 1971. In his decision, he said that although Mrs Clements' house had been left in the compulsory purchase order, he accepted the council's undertakings not to enforce the sale, and as to the price it would pay if she later changed her mind. Thus Mrs Clements was enabled to carry out her determination that 'come hell or high water,' she would not move.

As work proceeded, fate had other ideas. On the afternoon of June 29, 1973, a 60 feet high mobile crane was set up in Serpentine Road. It had come to dismantle one of

Building Barclays House: a masterpiece of organisation by the contractors, who had very little space in which to manoeuvre on the island site.

the tower cranes on the building site. As it took the weight of the tower crane's jib, one of the struts supporting the mobile crane sank into the road, and it overbalanced. The driver jumped from his cab. The crane and jib sheared through the roofs of three houses in Serpentine Road with a sickening crash. For a few moments the horror of the scene was obscured by the massive cloud of dust which rose from the wrecked houses. As the dust cloud drifted slowly away, blanketing Wimborne Road and bringing traffic to a stop, the full extent of the disaster was unveiled.

Although the roofs and first floors of the houses were shattered, most walls at ground floor level were intact. As the worried staff of John Laing, the main contractors, searched the wreckage for survivors, they found only Mrs Ellen Simmons (81), who lived with Mrs Clements, her daughter. She had been ironing in a back room and survived uninjured, indeed, unperturbed. She remarked to her rescuers that she hoped the crash 'had not rocked off all the apples from our trees, for they were loaded!'

What might so easily have been a fatal tragedy proved to be a near-miraculous escape. Mrs Simmons was able to confirm that there had been no one else in Mrs Clements' house. One of the other houses, used by the contractors as a site office, had been empty, but it was some time before it was confirmed that Millie Sheppard - who was 77 that day - and her blind sister Freda (73), of 23 Serpentine Road, had both been out visiting their sister.

The Town Clerk, who was on holiday, heard of the accident on the BBC national news at his hotel. The Council and the bank hurriedly arranged alternative accommodation for the two homeless families. The elderly Sheppard sisters considered the accommodation they were offered in Tatnam to be too far from their family. Barclays Bank hired a suite for them at the Dolphin Hotel.

Both owners wanted their houses rebuilt exactly as they had been. The Sheppard sisters had lived in their house since it was built in 1910, and blind Miss Freda knew every nook and cranny of her home. Mrs Clements reaffirmed her determination, expressed at the public inquiry, to remain in her house 'through hell and high water.' There was great public sympathy for their plight. Laing's site manager declared that if he was allowed to, he would take workmen off the site to rebuild the ruined homes: but wrangles between insurers stood in the way. The homeless were embroiled in a situation which involved three or four insurance companies and at least two firms of loss adjusters. Mr and Mrs Clements were told by their own insurers that they were not covered because the damage was not caused by a vehicle registered for road use. The insurers for Laings refused to admit liability, although they did admit that 'the law isn't designed to cope with sudden emergencies like this.' The insurers of the mobile crane suggested that the Corporation might be liable, because the road had given way underneath one of the struts. The only way in which the Corporation had expected to be involved was in making a claim itself for damage to the road.

In his role as solicitor for Mr and Mrs Clements, Alderman Adrian Greenwood was indignant, when it looked as though they would have to battle for every penny of compensation. 'This is not just a nice legal matter which we lawyers can spend months arguing about,' he said, 'but a matter which is causing Mr and Mrs Clements great anguish.'

Though Barclays House was completed without any further mishaps, there had never been any hope that it would be ready before the dissolution of the old Borough Council under the local government reforms of 1974. It was left to the new council to see the project brought to completion.

Those who assembled for the formal opening ceremony on January 27, 1976, were very different from those who first envisaged and implemented the plans to relocate much of the operations of Barclays Bank DCO to Poole. Only one of the two officials responsible for the siting and erection of the building had survived. Barclays Bank DCO had been engulfed by Barclays Bank, its principal shareholder, and renamed Barclays Bank International. Poole Corporation, which encouraged and facilitated the move, had been dissolved, and the chief officers who were intimately involved in all early aspects of the building's approval and construction had retired. As well as

Completion of Barclays House was a major step in the transformation of the Longfleet end of the town centre, into which it was successfully blended by the completion of other commercial and business developments.

members and officers of the new Council, the bank invited the former Town Clerk, Deputy Town Clerk, Borough Architect and Borough Engineer to the opening ceremony. It was performed by Antony F Tuke, Chairman of Barclays Bank International. Guests were entertained to lunch in the restaurant on the top floor of the building, with its panoramic views across a much transformed town.

It was a town which Barclays House itself would do much to transform, and initial public reaction to the nine-storey building was that it overpowered the surrounding ones. Its owners were quick to suggest that in the course of time it would settle much less obtrusively into the landscape. They maintained that it was not, as many believed, the town's tallest building. 'There are several ten storey blocks of flats near the harbour and a nurses' hostel which is prominently situated on high ground. The chimney of Poole power station is 325 feet and the boiler house 120 feet.'

LOCAL GOVERNMENT SERVICES

EDUCATION

In 1963, Poole's Committee for Education was desperately short of accommodation for its 5,820 primary school pupils. There were 161 classrooms having more than 30 pupils, 108 of them with over 36 to a classroom. What was more, six of these primary schools had been built before 1903 and could not be brought up to current standards. It was a similar situation in secondary schools.

Even if the Committee had been free to build more schools, it would have taken years to rectify the position. Far from having a free hand, it was subject to the overall control of a Government under pressure to restrict expenditure. Local ratepayers, meanwhile, were restive at the rising rate bill, much of it due to the cost of education.

On top of these restraints, Poole's school population of 12,586 in 1963 had risen 21% by 1968 (and its costs by 29%), and was still rising by over 500 pupils a year. Thus the position in primary schools, so far from improving, got worse as the 'bulge,' the dramatic increase in births during the immediate post-war years, worked its way through Poole schools. After 1970, it was the turn of the Technical College to try to contend with increased numbers.

Between 1960 and 1974, when the school population had risen to some 17,000, the committee had managed to build eleven new primary schools, four secondary schools, including two grammar schools, and Winchelsea School, for pupils with learning difficulties. It had also extended many schools, added temporary classrooms, and provided mobile classrooms to move from school to school as demand required.

The times, however, were not propitious for quiet progress. Inflation raised its inevitable stresses. Teachers' salaries, negotiated nationally, were a constant source of quarrels and publicity. The National Union of Teachers, to which 30% of Poole teachers belonged, was particularly active in pressing for a salary rise to reflect what it claimed was their greater professional standing. It was quite prepared to call a strike. In 1967, it chose Poole as an area in which members refused to supervise school dinners or collect contributions to their cost (then 1/- [5p] a meal). In December 1969, NUT members began a strike that effectively closed 13 classes in Poole schools. The following month, 1,000 children had to stay away from school.

The Government was in a dilemma over the spiralling costs of education, just as future governments would be over the health service. In both instances, public sympathy seemed mainly to be on the side of the employees. In Poole, this was fostered

Arthur Ingham, Borough Education Officer

Alderman Miss Jeanne Bisgood, Chairman, Committee for Education.

by the NUT writing a letter to 10,000 parents outlining its case. On the other hand, ratepayers felt aggrieved at Poole's increasing rate demands, which rose from a total of £1,272,729 in 1965 to £2,350,000 in 1970. There was a demand for increased grants from the Government. Compromises were eventually reached, but rarely with good grace or a settled policy with which both sides could feel happy.

In May 1970, there was another national crisis as, again, great shortages of solid fuel arose. The Council was informed that it could rely on no more than 50% of its supplies of coke or coal for that year and none for the following year. The Borough Engineer's electrical department was rapidly seconded to convert the heating systems of 13 schools to use off-peak electricity. By the autumn of that year it had also installed this new form of heating in the Parks Department nurseries and two Corporation depots.

The Council itself had its own long drawn out quarrel with the Government. It arose from the demand in October 1965, to prepare and submit plans for education in the borough to change to a comprehensive system. John Cleave, the Headmaster of Poole Grammar School, had anticipated the request in a speech demanding 'Hands off the Grammar Schools' the year before.

It was a theme tacitly accepted by a majority of teachers as well as the Committee for Education. In the following years a number of reports were produced on the subject, all critical of the system. Eventually, under pressure from Dorset County Council, which had accepted comprehensive education for county schools, a compromise plan was finally proposed for a Sixth Form College adjoining Poole Technical College.

'It's goodbye to Poole and Parkstone Grammar Schools in about a year's time,' reported the *Poole and Dorset Herald.* 'Poole Grammar School will become Canford Heath School and Parkstone, Broadstone School.'

The Government refused to accept Poole's compromise. Its patience was exhausted. It would not approve the building of any more schools in Poole until it had received 'a concrete plan' to implement a system of comprehensive education in the borough. When the minute of the Committee for Education came before the Council in which it appeared to have capitulated to the Government's wishes, there were cries of 'Giving in to blackmail.' Councillor Fred Rowe proposed a motion that the Council would not recognise any plan for comprehensive education as binding upon it, as it had been made under duress and 'after being rammed down our throats.' His motion was lost by only 18 votes to 13!

In November 1970, before there had been time to do anything practical about the plan, Mr Cleave was able to tell the Committee that, following a General Election, the threat to Grammar Schools 'had been removed.'

The official opening of the new premises of Poole Grammar School by Princess Margaret took place in October, 1966. With a lively council and community, and a sharp local newspaper, such an event could become the subject of controversy. National and local economies were in the 'stop' phase of Government 'stop-go' policies aimed at overcoming recurring financial problems. While some factions in the town could complain that too much was being spent on the princess's visit, others complained about not spending enough!

The 300 local members of the Boilermakers' Union asked that the Government's 'squeeze' should also apply to the lunch in honour of the Princess. Poole Trades Council, representing three thousand trade unionists, declared they were not anti-royalist, but it was the wrong time to squander public funds when the Government freeze had led to agreed pay increases being cancelled.

The Committee for Education had chosen a simple plaque at a cost of £39 to commemorate the opening of the school by the Princess. The school Governors were incensed that they had not been consulted and that the plaque did not even bear the Borough Coat of Arms. The plaque chosen by the Committee 'looks like the plaque outside HM Prisons' complained Councillor Jock Purdie. The committee's members were quite unrepentant. 'If the school governors want a different plaque, they can pay for it,' said one.

None of this controversy was taken over

Councillor Jock Purdie

into the Princess's visit. She came to Poole with a reputation of sometimes being a difficult guest, but was charming and agreeable to everyone involved in what to her must have been a very routine performance. She was expected to reflect in some way the jubilation of the local community at the belated replacement of their local Grammar School.

Certainly, Poole's Mayor at the time, Alderman Ronald Hart, must have seemed a refreshing change from the usual round of obsequious first citizens. With no inhibitions, be chatted with her, over lunch at the Municipal Buildings, almost as if they were old friends. He was horrified to find that Her Royal Highness had never been in a supermarket. He even suggested that she should stay in Poole overnight so that he could take her round Tesco's store the next day.

Even before this *tête á tête*, reporters covering the Princess's most successful visit were, as usual, looking for a new angle. They discovered that the Town Clerk had asked Ernest Gale, the Parks Superintendent, to hide the unsightly contractor's hut left outside the main entrance to the Grammar School with a couple of trees.

The local press seized upon it another example of unnecessary expense - and, by implication, of the obsessive attention to detail that often accompanies a Royal visit. Councillor Rowe, chairman of the Parks Committee, was asked at the next meeting of the Council what the cost had been. He replied that it had cost nothing, and refused to answer any more questions on the matter. His colleagues were left to wonder how it could have been done without a charge being raised somewhere in the Council's accounts. The Town Clerk found out that Councillor Rowe paid the cost himself!

The many developments carried out in those years had rarely been without controversy. Southern Television awarded the town a dubious accolade. It chose Poole for the first of a new series of programmes in which local government would be probed, with no punches pulled. The reason, the programme makers explained, was that Poole's controversies were among the most frequently featured on television of any town in the region.

Much less controversial was the act of generosity by a wealthy Bournemouth landowner, Miss Edith Cooper-Dean, which saved Uplands private school in Sandecotes Road, Parkstone. In 1972, its owners, the Church Education Corporation, decided to close Uplands, which had existed since the turn of the century, and sell the nine-acre site for housing development. The Edith Cooper-Dean Foundation bought the site for a six-figure sum. Part it was sold for development, but three acres, including the school buildings, were leased back to a new board of trustees, who continued to run it as a day school for girls. Miss Cooper-Dean also offered to spend up to £100,000 on improvements to the buildings. The school's new bursar was former borough councillor Geoffrey Adams.

HOUSING

By 1964 the Council had built 4,560 houses and flats since the war, and 415 were in various stages of construction. The Estates Committee reached the stage when it was able to offer accommodation to all married couples with two children, and often to those with one child. The Committee decided that, with the worst of the post-war housing crisis over, its policy should be reviewed.

The first change was to offer local industry up to 100 council houses for trained key personnel. The Manager of the Labour Exchange suggested such a scheme to the Council. She had over 50 vacancies for key workers who could not be recruited locally. After discussion with the Labour Exchange, the Chamber of Commerce and the Trades Council, a scheme was agreed. In cases where the Manager of the Labour Exchange certified that a vacancy was not able to be filled locally, and the company certified that employment of the key worker would enable it to employ other workers, a Council house would be offered to the successful applicant. The company would be responsible for the payment of an enhanced rent to ensure there was no loss to the housing account. At first the Council demurred but, the following year, it agreed to the scheme.

When it was reviewed five years later, the Committee felt it had been a success. The working population of the town had increased from 33,000 to 38,000. The proportion of the rates payable by industry had risen quite substantially, despite a great increase in private building.

Douglas Bush, Housing Manager

In the ensuing years the Committee considered a series of reviews submitted to it by Douglas Bush, the Housing Manager. One of its early decisions was that it would build no more large estates.

Building large estates in the desperate conditions after the second world war was the quickest and cheapest way to provide accommodation. In 1966, the Committee decided that having completed five such estates, Bourne (456 dwellings), Trinidad (325), Alderney (388) and Waterloo (750), Turlin Moor (planned for 836 dwellings) would be its last large estate. Future estates would comprise about 200 dwellings. Care would be taken to provide a variety of sizes of houses and flats. This last decision arose from the rather startling discovery that 80% of existing properties were three bedroomed, when the average number in a family had dropped to only three. The survey also showed that 359 tenants were living in accommodation with at least two bedrooms unused.

Pre-fabricated bungalows in Oakdale, which had helped to combat the post-war housing shortage, were reaching the end of their life.

Another disturbing finding was that the number of warden serviced bungalows or flats for the elderly in 1964 was only 45. It was estimated that 29% of Poole's 100,000 population was of pensionable age. A calculation made by the Housing Manager assumed that 70% of the elderly were able to fend for themselves, that 20% of them could cope with some help, and that half of these would be looked after by their families or would refuse any help. That left a balance of up to 1,000 persons who, ideally, should not live alone. A further 250 elderly people were not capable of looking after themselves and would need the help of county council or voluntary bodies' nursing homes. A similar number would need full medical or psychiatric help by the Hospital Management Committee.

As a result the Committee decided to accelerate the provision of its warden assisted dwellings. In the following ten years it provided 631 units on twenty sites chosen so that tenants did not have to move from districts with which they were familiar.

The committee was not alone in responding to this need. The Municipal and Owen Carter Trustees, with government and council help, provided 28 bungalows at Hamworthy. The Hanover Housing Trust was providing 28 units at Canford Heath and 24 on the site of a large house near Poole Hospital. Help the Aged built 18 units in Kingston Road on the site of the old Territorial Hall. Poole Lions Club, of which Geoffrey Hopkinson, the Borough Architect, was founder President, built 12 units in Garland Road. The Inskip Housing Association planned 25 units at Turlin Moor, and the Abbeyfield Society a home for eight elderly persons in the Penn Hill area.

Many substantial three and four-bedroomed council houses were built in Poole during the post-war years. It was a problem for the Council to encourage proud tenants whose families had left home to move into smaller and more manageable accommodation.

For the estimated 250 persons who were not inactive, but could not look after themselves, the County Council provided Alexandra House, Dorset House, and Elizabeth House, each to accommodate 55 persons, and Belmont House for the blind and partially sighted. Another home was proposed at Constitution Hill.

The hospital service provided for those who required full geriatric or psychiatric care with wards at St Leonards, the old US Military Hospital near Ringwood, and at Alderney Hospital, the Corporation's old infectious diseases hospital.

The Committee issued a pamphlet to encourage the elderly to move into more appropriate accommodation. Among its advice was the reminder that 'one heart attack or blood pressure could render the garden a nightmare...if the doctor says no gardening...be sensible and move to a flat. A window box can be fun.'

It urged them not be afraid of housing problems as they grew old. Private, local authority and other providers 'have now awakened to the special needs of each group and we shall not fail you.'

In the intervening years the Corporation continued to build houses at a reduced rate of some 200 a year. Following the new policy, smaller estates were established at Fleets Lane and Creekmoor.

Despite the Council's energetic council house building programme, the majority of its members were politically in favour of home ownership. To this end the Council adopted powers under the Housing Act, 1956, to make 50% grants to owners of older properties who were willing to install any of the 'standard amenities' of a bath, wash basin, hot water system, water closet and food store.

In 1965 the Government made it compulsory for local authorities to operate this system, as well as giving them power to insist upon landlords ensuring that these amenities were provided. The Council's preliminary estimate, as it started to carry out a survey of properties, was that up to 8,000 of Poole's 32,000 houses might be affected. Happily, the figure proved to be much lower, and the work was completed well inside the first estimate of ten years.

Another facet of the Corporation's policy of promoting home ownership was its operation of the Small Dwellings Acquisition Act to give mortgages to prospective owners of smaller properties; to purchasers of property needing refurbishment, such as the old houses in the Precinct; or to purchasers who preferred a fixed rate of interest, rather than the variable rates of Building Societies.

However, in 1970, the Government began its programme of promoting home ownership by allowing local authorities to sell council houses to sitting tenants. The Council, at the end of the war, owned nearly 100 odd houses, scattered round the borough. In the flurry to obtain accommodation quickly, the Corporation had acquired a further 300 or so houses erected by builders on small plots of land which they owned. By 1970 the Corporation had already sold 254 of these houses and was only too willing to sell the rest. Apart from that, even though the Council was predominantly Conservative, no dissenting voice was raised when it decided not to sell any of the houses on its estates.

When in 1973 the Government pressed the Council to reconsider its policy, the Borough Treasurer reported that each new house built by the Corporation to replace one sold at the price suggested by the Government, would cost it an extra £4,550. The Council had no hesitation in reaffirming its previous decision. It replied to the Minister that it agreed home ownership should be encouraged, but further encouragement was unnecessary in Poole. There was a wide range of private houses for sale, and ample funds were available for their purchase   There were financial disadvantages to the Council and the tenant in the purchase of a council house.

The Council had been concerned for years with the problems caused by 'gipsy' encampments at Canford Heath, Alderney Heath and other heathland areas. Under the Poole Corporation Act, 1961, it had power to make an order declaring it an offence to station a caravan for human occupation on open heathland. Before doing so, the Corporation decided to establish encampments to which the 'gipsies' could move. Public outcry led the Committee to reverse early proposals for a camp site.

Eventually, the Corporation found a site on Mannings Heath which, it felt, could offend no householders, but it did offend the landowner, Lord Wimborne. It therefore needed a public inquiry and a compulsory purchase order before three and a half acres of land could be secured. Here, a permanent camp for 22 families (82 people) was established in 1971. The camp provided a hard-standing for the caravans, a store, toilet,

The Council in 1973 saw financial disadvantages in selling Council houses to sitting tenants

electricity and laundry facilities, as well as a car space, at a rental of £2.25 per week. Even this site, however, did not accommodate all the gipsy families encamped on the heath, and a temporary site was provided for a further 28 families on Alderney Heath at a rental of £1.50. That year 60 families were turned off the heath and the considerable task of clearing it of debris could begin.

CANFORD HEATH

In November 1963, Dame Evelyn Sharp, permanent secretary to the Ministry of Housing and Local Government, officially opened the first house to be completed on Poole Borough Council's housing development at Canford Heath.

The visit gave the chief officers a chance to acquaint Dame Evelyn with Poole's ambitions, most of which would require her Department's approval. A few of the more politically oriented members of the Council thought a politician, not a civil servant, should have been invited. Dame Evelyn, herself a very outspoken woman, would have been amused, rather than irritated, to know this, for she was at least equally critical of politicians. She was, for instance, scathing of her current political master, the Minister of Housing and Local Government, who, she said, was forever urging her to produce a 'popular' measure which he could introduce.

Dame Evelyn Sharp officially opens the show house on Canford Heath.

Dame Evelyn duly declared the first Canford Heath house open in the presence of the Mayor, Sheriff and members of the Committee, praising the Council for its action. In the evening she addressed a packed council chamber, with officers filling the seats of three or four absent members.

Councillor Geoffrey Adams was one of those who disapproved of the visit. He underwent traumatic experiences as a prisoner of war of the Japanese, drafted to work on building the Burma railway, and had a strong antipathy to any expense which he thought wasteful. At the Council meeting following Dame Evelyn's visit, he asked Alderman Lloyd-Allen, Chairman of the Finance Committee, what the visit had cost. The Chairman, feeling that the visit had been most successful, testily replied that the cost to the Corporation had been £9 4s 2d, plus up to £5 for paper and binding of a brochure. Transport was provided by his own car and that of the Town Clerk. They would not dream of claiming any recompense. 'How many hours of officers' time?' persisted Councillor Adams. Alderman Lloyd-Allen snapped back that a time-sheet was not kept. 'The time incurred on the visit was less than the time and paper work used by the Corporation in answering questions of this nature,' he added.

What Councillor Adams did not know was that in the hurry to complete the first home in time for Dame Evelyn's visit, it had been built in the wrong place. The builders, Ruddock and Meighan, had had to pull down a two-bedroomed open plan bungalow and rebuild it!

RUDDOCK AND MEIGHAN LIMITED

Announce the Opening of the

SOUTH CANFORD HEATH SHOW HOUSE

on

THURSDAY, 7th NOVEMBER at 2.0p.m.

FITTED KITCHEN · CENTRAL HEATING · LANDSCAPED GARDENS

When you buy ℞ ▲▲ you buy QUALITY

TWO BEDROOM End of Terrace House	·	TWO BEDROOM Semi-Detached House	·	THREE BEDROOM Detached House
£2,990		**£3,190**		**£3,890**
THREE BEDROOM Detached Bungalow	·	TWO BEDROOM Detached Bungalow	·	THREE BEDROOM Detached H
£3,790		**£3,490**		**£4,790**

Eleven different types to choose from

Shortly afterwards, the builders were completing one new house a day. Properties were selling well, at £2,990 for a two-bedroom house at the end of a terrace, and £4,790 for a three-bedroom detached house. By the end of the year, Peter Coles, a partner in Fox and Sons, the estate agents, reported that he had sold 85 of the properties.

Poole Trades Council, representing several thousand trade union members in Poole, complained that the houses were too dear. To afford to buy one, said the Secretary, a purchaser would need an income of at least £18 a week. Only 600 of his members earned that much. Compared with a national average wage of £15 8s 0d, it meant that a man would have to work overtime, or his wife would have to work, to afford a house. The Trades Council resolved to raise a mass protest. It claimed that although a responsible group of officials was trying its utmost to make a scheme work for the benefit of the general ratepayers, the original policy had been side-tracked. This was that a £25 deposit and 100% mortgage would put home ownership within the financial reach of those already on the housing waiting list.

The Council could not sell land or property at less than a price that the District Valuer agreed, which meant selling at market value. Indeed, it had never promised that every family would be able to afford property on Canford Heath. The Council appreciated that it had to continue to produce rented accommodation and was continuing to build council houses as fast as the Government permitted.

By the end of 1964, the bulk of the property in Stage 1 of the development, 59 houses and 68 bungalows, had been built. The Corporation offered 48 plots on Stage 2 for individual purchase, as it had promised. Only five applications were made for these plots. Two were from applicants who, it was adjudged, could not afford the repayments on the likely mortgage. The Corporation compromised by offering an area of Stage 2 to the Hanover Housing Association and granting it a 100% mortgage to those on the waiting list wishing to buy a house.

By 1970 the estate had taken on its final shape. All five stages had been sold and 350 houses completed. The 48 acres of the sixth stage were split between Taylor Woodrow Homes and Carlton Homes. The developers carried on the Corporation's early policy of naming the roads after distinguished members of aircrews during the second world war, such as Lynn Road, Calder Road, Kellaway Road and Verity Crescent. The houses in this part of the estate were the first in Poole to be designed in metric standards. At Carlton's invitation, Wing Commander D E Bennett opened the show house in April 1971.

Taylor Woodrow in 1970 completed the shops and car park in the centre of the estate, with provision for a church, a library, doctor's and dentist's surgeries, and a public house. A Waitrose supermarket and most of the other 12 shops had been opened. The Presbyterian Church was completed in June, 1970. The temporary hall in which it held its earlier services was bought by the Corporation and let to Canford Heath Residents' and Community Association.

Canford Heath Middle School opened in September 1970. The population of the estate had grown so fast, and the approvals for building the school had taken so long, that by the time it opened, it already needed additional temporary classrooms.

The 'Fighter Pilot' public house and skittle alley were opened by Group Captain Douglas Bader, VC. It was most appropriate for him to perform the ceremony, even though he was a teetotaller, for he was also the most famous of RAF fighter pilots. Eldridge Pope, the owners, had taken great trouble in the design and fittings, even to the extent of having a special carpet woven depicting the roundels, propellers, and silhouettes of Spitfire fighter planes. Unfortunately, a more recent Spitfire was used as a model. The carpet showed the fighter with four propeller blades, instead of the original three. This fact was not lost on the Group Captain. In his opening speech, he said: 'If, on a particularly boozy night, you could remove one of the blades from the carpet, I would be very grateful indeed!'

With the estate in process of completion, the Borough Treasurer estimated that the receipts from sales would produce a credit balance of £313,000 after allowing for a contribution of £150,000 towards the new central library and £33,000 towards the cost of the Sports Centre. What was more, the cost of the offsite roads and sewers had been met by the Council.

The population of Poole was still rising strongly. The South East Dorset and South West Hampshire Study of 1967 was designed to deal with problems of the future growth of Poole, Bournemouth and Christchurch. It estimated that the population of these areas would rise to 310,000 by the year 2001. It recommended that planning approvals should be given well in advance to allow this increase to take place in a coherent fashion.

The Council therefore decided to submit a planning application to develop 540 acres of the heath lying south of the escarpment which ran west to east across it. The plan proposed building two main traffic routes. There would be a primary route,

Getting his hands on another "gong" – Group Captain Douglas Bader, VC, inspects the Mayor's badge at the opening of the Fighter Pilot public house, Canford Heath.

running off Old Wareham Road northwards to the east of Phase 1 of the development. The other road would run from a point in Gravel Hill opposite Dunyeats Road, along the line of the old Award Road, to join the new route from Old Wareham Road at a point opposite Wallisdown Road.

Allowing for land required for these roads, as well as a new road serving the estate from Darby's Corner, estate roads, schools, open spaces and another community centre, some 340 acres would be left for residential development. The estate's population, then estimated at 4,500, would rise by a further 14,000.

Encouraged by the success of the development so far, council members were surprisingly uncritical of the proposal to buy such a large area of land. They quite readily agreed a price of £7.6 million, which the District Valuer considered 'cheap.' Perhaps they were reassured by newspaper estimates that it would ultimately be worth some £25 million.

The Ministry, however, did not so readily agree. It declared that it had no powers for it to agree to the Council undertaking such a venture. The officers persisted. Apart from the magnitude of the scheme, they asked, what was different from Phase 1? In that instance, the Corporation borrowed money under the Housing Acts, making sure that the housing account was fully reimbursed. At a final meeting with a very senior official at the Ministry the purchase was agreed on the same basis, as there was by then a Bill before Parliament to provide for such an undertaking. Even if it agreed in principle, the Ministry could not sanction such a large loan in one tranche: it would have to be phased over some years. After further negotiations with Lord Wimborne it was agreed to defer a portion of the purchase price, with the Corporation paying 4% interest on the outstanding amount. This arrangement was easy to accept when it was having to pay 7% on other new loans.

The time was approaching when the Government, far from increasing the powers of local authorities, would set about reducing them. The Bill that would have clarified the Council's powers was not passed by Parliament until a few years later. When the Community Land Act was passed, the Canford Heath development became the forerunner of the type of development envisaged in the Act.

Before the reorganised Council took over in April, 1974, development of Phase 2 of Canford Heath proceeded well, and seemed to be set for a successful conclusion. The new Council was left to weather a difficult period of recession in the housing market, when it decided to sell no more land at prices then ruling. However, the interest and repayment of the loans continued, and this led to dire warnings in the District Auditor's report on the last years of the old Council's tenure, which are briefly referred to in the Postscript.

DRAINAGE

Poole Borough Council had been warned in 1956 that Ministerial approval of plans to divert sewage from Poole Bay could be given only in stages. Separate applications for every stage of the work resulted in recurring delays while public inquiries were held. There was then a delay while the Minister considered the inspector's report. The timing of the announcement of his decision often depended more upon the recurring 'stop and go' crises in the country's finances than on the merits of the proposal.

In the periods of 'stop,' when the Government feared an overheating economy, approvals were not often issued; but, when it feared that a slump was developing, it would be anxious for new work to commence. This sometimes led the Ministry, just before the end of the financial year, to offer a loan sanction for approved work, on condition that the Council could complete a contract for it before April. The Borough Engineer and Borough Architect were always ready with contract documents prepared for dispatch, and thus obtained early approval for some contracts.

It became apparent that diversion of sewage was a greater undertaking than first envisaged. Even if approvals had been readily available, the work could never have been completed within the original time span. Many miles of sewers had to be laid, 18 new pumping stations constructed, and nine others extended and modernised There were also considerable delays in the supply of pumping equipment.

Moreover, sewage diversion was not the only problem in the period. Some of the developed areas of the town became flooded at periods of high rainfall, and intensive development spreading to low-lying areas created substantially increased flows of

Broadstone sewage disposal works.

surface water. New surface water sewers and pumping stations were required, some through difficult areas such as Poole station goods yard and under the railway, which could only be laid on Christmas Day. In Poole Park, to avoid the road between the lakes, the sewer had to be laid under the salt water lake.

A further delay was caused by the need for more land for the purification works. The land immediately to the west of the existing works, once part of Plainfield Farm, was owned by Dorset County Council and used for playing fields. The county council was not willing to convey land to the Corporation unless it could offer a suitable replacement. This could not be done until the Corporation could offer the county council an equivalent area of land at Canford Heath.

It was thus 1970 before the second purification works could be built, which brought the capacity up to dealing with a population of 100,000. By that time the Corporation had a ring of 44 pumping stations round the borough. They were all connected by a telemetric system of surveillance at a central control room, which dealt with 80% of the population.

The only areas of the town remaining to be dealt with were Sandbanks, Lilliput and Branksome Park. Large pumping stations were needed at Shore Road and Branksome Chine. It was decided that the stations in these prominent positions must be out of sight, and deep excavations were necessary to accommodate them. It was 1971 before the diversion of sewage from Poole Bay, a project once earmarked for completion in the early 1960s, was achieved.

Meanwhile, the Corporation laid sewers in the northern area of the borough, comprising Canford, Merley, and Bearwood, and connected them to the sewage works of Wimborne Urban District Council. This allowed the discontinuance of some 1,000 cesspools and pail closets in those areas.

WATER AND SEWERAGE SERVICES

Councillor Bob Hann

It was ironic that in 1971, the very year when Poole finally completed its sewage works, and abandoned sea outfalls, the Government decided to appoint regional water authorities to take over all responsibilities for water supply and sewage disposal.

Ten authorities were approved for England and Wales , with areas based on natural watersheds, regardless of existing local government boundaries. Poole was included in a region whose boundaries stretched from the Bristol Channel to the English Channel, and comprised the watersheds of Avon and Dorset, Bristol, and Avon and Somerset River Authorities.

It was decided that the changes would be made at the same time as the reform of local government. Under the timetable to achieve this, comments on the proposals had to be made by March, 1972. Then, just after the election of new district councils in June, 1973, 'shadow' regional authorities were to be set up. They were then to become operational on April 1, 1974, the same day as the new district councils.

Not only did Poole Borough Council lose its new sewage works and all responsibility for sewerage. It also lost its partial control of the local Water Board, whose 18 members included nine nominees of the Council, with Poole's Councillor Bob Hann as its chairman.

The loss of all responsibility for these services, in which members felt great pride, having spent much time and money on them, was felt as a great blow to the council.

TRANSPORT

The proliferation in the ownership of cars and lorries in the 1960s gradually changed the pattern of life. As the number of bus passengers fell, the Hants and Dorset bus company made frequent applications to raise fares. It sought to balance its books, even though higher fares tended to reduce the number of passengers even further.

British Rail had already felt the effect of the Beeching plan, which resulted in many branch lines being closed. In Poole there was a continuing concern that the line from Bournemouth to Weymouth, which cost the Government over £600,000 a year in subsidy, would be the next to go.

Top: The old Poole railway station.
Bottom: Poole's new railway station was considered a Spartan, windswept affair by comparison with the long covered platforms of the old one.

Robert Hawker, Borough Engineer

This fear increased when Poole station, demolished to make way for Towngate Bridge, was replaced by a much smaller station with greatly inferior facilities. The old station's covered platform of 180 feet was replaced by an open one of a mere 48 feet. The only access to the 'down' line was via a steep, utilitarian bridge, which offered no protection from wind or rain. In 1967, when electrification of the line ceased at Bournemouth, the service through Poole to Weymouth was continued by diesel train, and worries were somewhat abated.

The fears of Swanage, however, were well founded, for in 1969 the Minister announced that its branch line was to be closed. Traders and hotel proprietors were shocked, fearing loss of business to the town. Swanage Council wrote urgently requesting a meeting with the Minister to reconsider the decision, only to be told brusquely that he refused to receive a deputation.

For Poole, the growing use of cars brought many problems. Roads became congested, some junctions became particularly dangerous, and accidents increased alarmingly, especially among pedestrians and cyclists.

On Gravel Hill, Broadstone, in 1965, there had already been a foretaste of the tragedy that could be wrought by the motor car, which the public would all too soon come to accept in an unnaturally matter-of-fact way. Between March and August of that year, five people were killed in three accidents. A Wimborne father lost two sons: one aged 22, in June, and another, aged 18. in August. On both occasions the news was broken to him by a Dorset policeman whose own daughter had been killed in a head-on crash on Gravel Hill in March 1965. The collisions were blamed on dips in the road which made it possible for drivers to lose sight of vehicles coming the other way. Robert Hawker, the Borough Engineer, ordered the painting of double white lines on the carriageway.

In 1968, twenty people were killed in road accidents in Poole. The following year, though deaths were reduced to six, there were 1,495 traffic accidents in which 772 people were injured, 278 of them seriously.

Poole had appointed a Road Safety Officer as early as 1956, and an Accident Prevention Committee that included police and residents' organisations. Later, Poole Junior Accident Prevention Council was established, on which nearly every school in the town was represented, and a Poole Women's Committee for Road and Home Safety, whose members were appointed by local women's associations. The Accident Prevention Committee campaigned to improve safety on the road, setting up safe cycling and motor-cycling courses and Advanced Drivers' Courses for motorists. It also advised on the siting of twenty-nine pedestrian crossings which were provided as soon as the council was empowered to do so.

To try to mitigate the growing number of road casualties, various kinds of crossing points were established to give pedestrians right of way across busy roads. The rising danger from parked cars was tackled by imposing waiting restrictions. By the late 1960s, over 200 such orders had been made. To enforce the orders, three full-time Traffic Wardens were appointed. In summer, three further wardens were employed to cover Sandbanks, Canford Cliffs and Branksome Chine. It did mean, though, that if parking was to be banned on roads around busy centres of the town, off-street car parks had to be provided. By 1968, a programme was well under way, which included multi-storey parks at the Arndale shopping centre, Hill Street and Old Orchard in the more congested area of the Old Town.

In 1968 there was capacity for 800 cars in the Corporation's car parks. Although at first they were free to the motorist, there was a mounting charge to the ratepayer which, that year, amounted to £15,000. The Council therefore proposed to make a charge for using its car parks.

Many Poole motorists were horrified at the proposal. One motorist raged that *Poole Council want to charge me ten shillings to keep my job.* The Chamber of Trade claimed that car parking should be free for the first one and a half hours, and an Anti-Car Park Charges Committee was formed. Five thousand leaflets, printed in patriotic colours of red, white and blue, were placed on the windscreens of cars with a ready-printed letter, addressed to the Town Clerk, complaining that parking facilities were already paid for in the rates, and an appeal was made to the Minister against the order imposing the charges. At a public inquiry, Mr Raymond Ashdown, who appeared on behalf of the Anti-Car Park Charges Committee, presented a petition signed by 1,140 residents.

The Minister decided that the proposed order was reasonable and gave his approval to charges of threepence (1.25p) for up to two hours, sixpence (2.5p) for two and a half hours, ninepence (3.75p) for up to three hours, and two shillings (10p) for up to four hours. Even with charges levied from July 1968, it was estimated that by 1970 there would be a loss to the rate fund of £31,600, due to the cost of providing further parking, especially in multi-storey car parks. The number of parking spaces would by then have risen to a total of 2,696. The council deferred increasing charges until after decimal currency was introduced in 1971. It then increased them by more than 50%, to 2p for up to one hour; 4p up to two hours, and 6p for up to three hours.

Despite the attention given to trying to safeguard pedestrians and cyclists, the growing number of motor vehicle accidents was also causing great concern. In 1970 there were 669 road casualties in Poole, about the same number as in the previous five years. Of these casualties, 299 were in accidents involving cars. Three were killed and 82 seriously injured. Accidents involving motor-cyclists and their pillion passengers caused 140 injuries, including two fatalities and 47 cases of serious injury. Of 85 pedal cyclists involved in accidents, 30 were seriously hurt: but, as could be anticipated, pedestrians involved in road accidents fared the worst. Of the 145 pedestrians involved,

Commercial Road with the Civic Centre roundabout in the background. A gyratory system would be needed to cope with increasing traffic.

eight were killed (including two children) and 43 seriously injured (including 23 children).

Road junctions were one of the main sources of danger, and each had its own problems. Though traffic lights could eliminate danger where roads crossed at right angles, and be satisfactory even where junctions were five-legged, such as at Penn Hill Corner, it was thought that at intersections such as Fleets Bridge, Hunger Hill, Wallisdown Road and Waterloo Road, large roundabouts were needed, and that at County Gates and the Municipal Buildings, only a new gyratory system would suffice.

The increased volume of traffic meant that main roads in the borough became unable to cope with it safely. Sometimes, a widening scheme sufficed, such as making Old Wareham Road and a stretch of Waterloo Road into dual carriageways, but some entirely new roads were also required, such as the construction of the new West Street in Old Poole.

While the extension of Fleets Lane, across what was then open ground, to join Fleets Bridge roundabout, elicited no opposition, other proposals for new roads met with great objection from residents who considered their amenities might be affected. One such scheme was the new road from Fleets Roundabout westward, by-passing Upton, proposed by Dorset County Council. A committee of protesters, which included some experienced Poole complainants, claimed, among other things, that it would affect turbary rights. Protesters obtained the support of the Commons, Open Spaces and Footpaths Society, and the quarrel was settled only when the county council agreed to provide 21 acres of land by way of compensation. The delay caused, of over a year, also delayed the opening of Upton House to the public, for the provision of a safe vehicle access depended on the construction of the by-pass.

Another new road, now part of Wessex Way, was proposed by Bournemouth Corporation to by-pass Westbourne, taking traffic from Bournemouth town centre to County Gates. It was now the turn of Poole Corporation to be an objector, and seek to delay the scheme until other roads designed to take westbound traffic from Westbourne had been built.

In 1970 there were 81 accidents in Ashley Road, Upper Parkstone, which caused injury to road users. Poole Corporation, which was already undertaking a series of safety measures, including traffic lights, lay-bys, no waiting orders and pedestrian crossings, considered that to encourage additional through traffic into Upper Parkstone would undo all its efforts. Be that as it may, Bournemouth went on with its proposal, and the new road was completed in 1972.

Meanwhile, Poole Corporation faced strong opposition to attempts to complete a new lateral road, connecting Lower Parkstone to Bournemouth, which had been part of the town's overall plan ever since Sir Patrick Abercrombie submitted his proposals for development to Bournemouth and Poole Corporations just after the second world war. In 1969 the Corporation proposed that the road should be put into the building programme. It would join Elgin Road via Compton Drive to Links Road, which in turn would be linked via Bury Road into Western Road. It was seen as a local collector road, which would benefit residents in those areas, by facilitating their access to Poole and Bournemouth and relieving some congestion in main roads. The reaction of many of those whom the road was intended to benefit was one of hostility, not gratitude. No less than 500 people attended a meeting designed to explain its purpose. The great majority were suspicious of the Corporation's intentions, feared a proliferation of lorries rushing through their neighbourhood, and cast an overwhelming vote against it. The council decided it had no great wish to force the issue, and quietly abandoned its decision to put it into the road building programme .

Meanwhile, the very weight of traffic continued to overwhelm the best efforts of the Government and local authorities to eliminate danger on the roads. Police tacitly abandoned most efforts to contain the speed of traffic in built up areas to 30mph. The Ministry suggested that in some roads the speed limit could safely be increased to 40 mph. The Superintendent at Poole reported that the average speed of traffic in some roads was already over 40 mph, and suggested five roads in the borough for which the limit could be raised. There was an immediate reaction from schools and the public against any relaxation of the limit. The Council, feeling that such a step might tend to increase average speeds even further, refused to alter any 30 mph limit in the town.

The Government introduced other measures designed to reduce accidents, such as an Act of Parliament which, in 1967, gave the police powers to breath-test drivers for alcohol, and to demand blood samples if the test proved positive. The first motorist to be convicted in Poole of the new offence of driving when the proportion of alcohol in the blood was in excess of the statutory limit appeared before the borough magistrates in November of that year. Fear of the new law had caused a few local organisations to cancel their annual dinners that autumn. Public house car parks acquired a deserted air, and the speed of most traffic in the town around closing time was voluntarily reduced to a steady 30 miles per hour. Later, to try to reduce the severity of injuries to motorists, it was made compulsory to wear seat belts.

These national and local efforts had some effect. In Poole, despite the increasing number of cars, the number of accidents did show a slight reduction over the years. There were, however, still over 600 accidents each year. Fifteen people were killed on roads in Poole in 1969; 13 in 1970, and seven in 1971. The total of serious injuries was never less than the 187 recorded in 1971 when the total of accidents reported, 622, at least showed some reduction.

REFUSE

Until 1967, Poole's refuse was incinerated at the refuse disposal works in Hatch Pond Road. The moistened dust was deposited as land-fill, and the clinker used in the foundations of roads. Each refuse collecting vehicle pulled an open trailer into which

The refuse pulverisation plant under construction.

Alderman Mrs Rene Montague

collectors put bundles of waste paper saved by many householders. It was baled at the works and sold as salvage, and the 1,709 tons collected in 1965 provided an income of £16,000. Tins and metals were extracted from the conveyor belt which fed the furnace. These were then compressed in the works' 100-ton press and sold.

In 1966, the Council decided to install pulverisation plant at Hatch Pond Road at a cost of £205,000. The paper was abstracted from the refuse on its way along the conveyor to the five-ton 'Fermascreen' tumbling drums which heated the refuse, breaking it down as it automatically segregated the tins and metals. At the end of this process the residue was a moist, fibrous material which had none of the disadvantages that arose when crude refuse was dumped on land with periodic coverings of earth. It provided an ideal material for land-fill, one which did not create the usual hazards of blown paper, smell, vermin or fire risks.

The plant, the second of its kind in the country to be commissioned, was formally opened by Alderman Fred Rowe in early 1967 and was successfully operated until 1974 when the duty of refuse disposal was transferred to the County Council.

Residue was used to fill a strip of Holes Bay adjoining land bought by the Corporation to the south of Fleets Lane, where a new road had been planned to run from Hunger Hill roundabout westwards. It was also used to fill low lying land near Fleets roundabout which was needed for a further widening of Old Wareham Road.

The most striking benefit of the new material was that it enabled the second and last stage of the reclamation of Baiter to be treated as a land-fill site, at a time when there was little likelihood of obtaining loan sanction to spend an estimated £46,500 for imported material. The Corporation was able to complete the reclamation with 250,000 cubic yards of residue and at the same time, save the cost of imported hard-core.

It was, perhaps, too much to hope that Poole's refuse disposal operations would escape the recurring strikes which afflicted much of Britain's industry in this period. In October, 1970, all refuse disposal workers were called out by their Union on a national strike to which the whole of the Corporation's workforce of 107 men responded.

The Corporation called upon residents to burn as much refuse as they reasonably could, and to store paper and other dry refuse in their garages or outhouses. It set up 40 collecting points round the borough to which residents were invited to bring other refuse, such as kitchen waste.

The refuse workers themselves were concerned at the possible health risk and offered to return to deal with any such danger, so long as independent contractors were not employed. Their representatives, however, took great exception to remarks made by Alderman Mrs Rene Montague, the Sheriff, who was also chairman of the Health Committee, which dealt with refuse disposal. She said it was absurd for Poole strikers to claim they were seeking to achieve a minimum wage of £16 10s 0d a week when the lowest paid among them was already receiving, with bonuses, £21 10s 0d a week. The men retorted that they had no quarrel with the Corporation, and had held no discussions with the management about wages, but were bound by solidarity with their Union and fellow workers to seek a minimum national basic wage.

The strike was settled during the following month by a manual workers' pay award which, when applied to the Poole workers, cost a further £500 a week.

CIVIL DEFENCE

During the early 1960s the hostility between Communist Russia and the West continued unabated. In 1960, the Russians shot down an American spy plane, and in 1962, when Khruschev, the Russian dictator, decided to station missiles in Cuba, the Cold War threatened to blossom into full-scale hostilities.

For many years it had been the responsibility of local authorities to establish and maintain a trained Civil Defence force. The Government actively encouraged this with financial aid as well as an on-going national campaign of publicity and recruitment. The bulk of the citizens of Poole, like many others in Britain, found it difficult to conceive that nations which so recently endured a war could begin another, and recruitment to the Civil Defence Corps was never easy. The Poole corps never exceeded 400 volunteers.

Happily, though, they became an active force, its members undertaking the long training periods in rescue, first aid, ambulance duties, care of the homeless, signals and intelligence. There were frequent exercises with other forces and local Territorials until it was believed this well-trained nucleus of personnel could be quickly expanded to deal with any national or local emergency,

Throughout this time, Alderman A B Haynes, chairman of the small Civil Defence Sub-Committee of the council, gave his active and enthusiastic support to the volunteers. A Civil Defence Club was formed and social occasions were organised under the patronage of 'AB.' The corps became a compact and energetic unit of which the town could be proud.

The Government decided in 1966 to abandon its national publicity campaign. Although it made no difference to the total strength of the Poole force, its members feared that it signalled a complete change of attitude by the Government to Civil Defence.

Their fears were soon realised. The last exercise that the corps carried out was to install the signals and communication systems for Poole Regatta that year. In 1967 the Government ordered a radical reduction in personnel. It resulted in the loss of three out of four of Poole's permanent staff, which brought an end to all training. Only the Civil Defence Officer himself remained, and then only for long enough to wind up the affairs of the corps.

To the chagrin of the Poole volunteers, the Government ordered the final abandonment of the Civil Defence organisation on March 31, 1967. Many members were unhappy with the impersonal, *Dear Sir or Madam* letter of thanks they received. They felt their arduous training and long service deserved better than that. Their feelings were only partially assuaged by a letter from the County Civil Defence Officer, to whom the duties had passed, thanking them and enclosing a message of thanks from the Queen.

'AB' Haynes was similarly offended that 'no one had told him that he was sacked' before his committee's functions were taken away. Later, perhaps, he received some consolation on being made a Member of the Order of the British Empire, in recognition of his efforts for Civil Defence.

WEIGHTS AND MEASURES

The Charter granted by Queen Elizabeth I in 1568 empowered the Burgesses of Poole to appoint an officer to check the weight and measurement of 'bread, wine and beer and all other sorts of victuals and weights.' Poole had operated a weights and measures service ever since.

The duties of the service were greatly extended over the years. It was still an important service, as was seen in the 258 cases of incorrectly labelled products reported in 1971. Its duty to ensure the correct measurement of petrol sold, for instance, was extended to the licensing and safe storage of the 11,000,000 gallons stored in the town and port during the late 1960s. The department was also responsible for the safety of explosives, including fireworks which were sold at some 100 shops and stores.

The greatest increase of its responsibilities was brought about by legislation in the late 1960s, especially the Trade Descriptions Act, 1968, which attained considerable

Geoffrey Roberts,
Chief Inspector of Weights and Measures

publicity as the 'Shoppers' Charter.' It was made a criminal offence to advertise or make representations about an article or service which were untrue. Poole residents took full advantage of their new rights. So many complaints were made that the department established a Consumer Complaints Service. It was kept busy looking into scores of complaints which ranged from alleged misdescriptions of second-hand cars, to the merits of package holidays and cosmetics.

In 1974, in the 400th year of its existence, the duties of the department were transferred to Dorset County Council. It was the only Poole service to be transferred which took with it the borough's chief officer. Geoffrey Roberts, who had been chairman of the Institute of Weights and Measures in 1971, took up his new duties, which covered the whole county of Dorset, in April, 1974.

WORKS DEPARTMENT

The Works Department of the Corporation was established in 1946 during the acute housing shortage which followed the ending of the war. Alderman Fred Reeves, the leader of the Labour party on the Council, persuaded the Council that such a department could produce houses expediently and cheaply. He was the leading advocate in the Corporation's case to the Ministry for permission to borrow the money necessary to establish the department. He was also chairman of the council committee overseeing the department from 1946 until his death in 1959.

The department was always treated as if it was an outside contractor. It was required to submit tenders to carry out work for the council or county council in the same way as private contractors, and it would only be awarded the contract if its tender price was the lowest received.

The department was first housed with the Borough Engineer's central depot in Wimborne Road, with its office in Commercial Road. In 1953 It was transferred to the old prison buildings in King Street. It won a considerable number of contracts to build council houses and flats, new schools and school extensions and many other buildings for the council, Dorset County Council and the Ministry of Works. It employed some 130 tradesmen and 14 apprentices and, in later years, had an annual turnover of about £300,000,

This figure also included a great deal of work in the maintenance and redecoration of schools, clinics, libraries, beach huts, beach cafes, sports pavilions, and public lavatories, as well as the 6,600 dwellings then owned by the Corporation.

Its existence was a thorn in the flesh of local building contractors. They claimed that it was unfair competition from a department set up with ratepayers' money, to which they had contributed. Its existence also offended the political sensibility of some Conservative members of the council. They were always alert to ensure that the arm's length basis of dealing with the department was maintained and that its finances were constantly watched. Their concern was heightened by stories of direct labour departments in other towns suffering horrendous losses.

As long as the department continued to comply with the strict conditions that had been laid down, and also make a profit, criticism was muted. Even members of the council who disapproved of its existence in principle became proud of its achievements.

By 1965 the department had repaid the loan raised for its establishment and contributed £35,000 of its profits to the relief of rates. Council members supporting it would ask the chairman of the Finance Committee to tell the council of the hidden extra amount which the department had saved by obtaining a tender, compared with what it would have cost to accept the second lowest figure. This extra 'saving' more than doubled the savings to the Council.

Council housing contracts were vital to the continued viability of the Works Department.

However, conditions were changing. Though the number of houses and flats allocated for the council to build was maintained in the earlier 1960s, the Corporation decided that, to maintain the population in the Old Town, it was necessary to provide flats in high-rise blocks. The department was not equipped to build multi-storey buildings, and could not compete for such contracts.

It still won contracts for council houses at Turlin Moor as well as the contract to build the new Poole Grammar School at Gravel Hill. By 1964, the worst of the housing crisis was over. The Corporation lost its extra allocation of houses for tenants displaced by slum clearance, and was told that its future allocation would not exceed 120 units a year.

One of the benefits of having the Works Department was shown in October 1966 when serious damage was caused by a freak whirlwind. Its workmen were switched to repairing property in Grove, Cranbrook, Haskells, Blackburn and Harford Roads. They also dealt with seafront damage to beach huts and railings.

This work delayed the completion of 131 houses which the Department had in contract at Turlin Moor. It was in a disadvantageous position to tender for further contracts because it was also heavily committed to complete the building of Poole Grammar School.

The future of the department became in doubt when the Government, despite the appeals of the Council, decreed that it would sanction the Council to build only 130 to 150 council houses a year in future. The Chief Officers reported that, for the Department to continue to be viable, it would have to win contracts to build at least 80 of these houses.

The Government had foreseen that local authority works departments would face difficulties with the decreased amount of council building. It relaxed its condition that one contract in every three had to be put out to open tender. It ordained that, in future, local authorities, once they had adopted financial safeguards, could award contracts to works departments without putting them out to open tender.

The Council had, in fact, never adopted the earlier freedom of only putting one contract in three out to tender. It had always insisted on all contracts being subject to tender, and it was quite unwilling to change its practice.

The Chief Officers reported that, if the Council was unwilling to adopt the new freedoms, the Works Department could hardly hope to be able to rely on continuity of work. Unless it was allocated a minimum of 80 houses a year to build, there was little alternative to shutting it down.

The council decided to close down the capital building side, to transfer a further £10,000 from its reserves into the rate fund, and to hold the balance of its reserves until its contracts to build 131 houses at Turlin Moor were completed. It made the Borough Engineer responsible for the completion of this contract, and reorganised the maintenance side of the department, transferring control to the Borough Architect with the assistance of the Estates Surveyor.

PLANNING

Geoffrey Hopkinson, Borough Architect

Planning consent to develop land usually added considerable value to it. On the other hand, owners of nearby property would often feel that they would be adversely affected, and this could frequently give rise to friction.

This was particularly so in Poole during the 1960s and early 1970s when the town was in a period of high activity and rapid expansion. During these years the Planning Committee received an average of well over 3,000 planning applications each year. The total rose to 4,242 in 1965 and thereafter was never less than 3,500. A survey of towns in the south demonstrated the strain imposed on the officers and members of the Planning Committee. It showed that Poole, with 27.9 applications per 1,000 population, received more than twice the proportion of any town in the survey. Reading received 9.5 applications per 1,000 population, Eastbourne 10.7 and Worthing 11.7.

The weight of applications presented the six members of the planning staff with great difficulties. It was not as though this was the total of their duties. They also had to investigate complaints of planning infringements, interview many personal callers at the office, and submit evidence to over twenty planning appeals each year.

It was no easier for the chairman and members of the Planning Committee. The meetings continued into the evening, and were increased to two a month and later to four every six weeks. For one of these meetings a coach was hired to deal with applications where members felt that a decision could only be made after inspecting the site.

It was, therefore, perhaps inevitable that some disputed decisions would erupt into public quarrels. One of these arose with a local businessman, Clifford Brewer, who had been a councillor from 1937-1939. He had been endeavouring to win planning permission for a block of flats in Fernside Road. The plans were strongly opposed by neighbouring residents in Alverton Avenue and Churchfield Road, who claimed they would be overlooked. Every application he had made since 1960 was refused, and in 1963 he lost an appeal to the Minister.

By 1965, when he made his second appeal, relations between Mr Brewer and the Council had become strained. Counsel for Mr Brewer told the public inquiry that there had been unreasonable opposition to his plans. For the Council, Bob Cass, the deputy Town Clerk, accused Mr Brewer of wasting the Ministry's time and asked for the

Alderman Herbert Ballam   *Alderman Leslie Miller*

Council to be awarded costs against him. Mr Brewer claimed to have a five-page list of cases where the Council had approved flats at much higher densities than his proposals.

Mr Brewer became particularly incensed by the Council's decision to allow a block of flats at 39 and 41, Parkstone Road, adjoining Saint Joseph's Convent, on the corner of Parkstone and Churchfield Roads. As Chairman of the Poole Group of the Civil Rights Association, he called a public meeting in the Library Hall in South Road, to discuss this approval and 'a long list of planning inconsistencies.' He was joined by Paul Smith, the dismissed Town Clerk of Bognor, who had formed the Local Government Reform Society. Mr Smith announced that he would be carrying out his own inquiry into the Parkstone Road decision.

Mr Brewer complained that the decision was somehow influenced by the fact that a planning officer who retired in 1964 had an interest in one of the sites; and that the height of the proposed building had been increased. He alleged that the building offended the daylight regulations so much that the convent had to whiten some of its windows to prevent occupants of the flats looking directly into it; that the building line in Churchfield Road had been ignored; and that, in any case, the building constituted an overdevelopment of the site.

Alderman Ballam, a member of the Planning Committee, attended the meeting. He accused Mr Brewer of 'the old smear technique of McCarthy,' but was unable to stem the torrent of criticism. Bill Foot, a Poole insurance broker, claimed he had been advised that a maximum of only three floors would be allowed when he was considering a development on the same site. This called forth a retort from Alderman Leslie Miller, a former chairman of the Planning Committee, which perhaps summed up the dilemma facing every disappointed developer: 'He should know that the Planning Committee changes from year to year - and so does our policy.'

The meeting carried a resolution calling for the permission to be revoked. Mr Brewer got no support for a further proposition calling for Geoffrey Hopkinson to be suspended from duty as Borough Architect pending the result of an inquiry by the Minister. A day or so later, Southern Television screened a debate on the subject in which the ex-Town Clerk of Bognor and Oscar Murton, Poole's MP, took part.

In December 1964, Clifford Brewer had written in much more strident tones to every Member of Parliament. His letter alleged that Poole solicitors objected to dealing with matters for their clients if they were likely to bring them into conflict with local government administrators. Alderman Adrian Greenwood, a local solicitor , and not a member of the Planning Committee, took great exception and issued a writ for libel. In 1966 at Hampshire Assizes, Mr Brewer made an unreserved withdrawal and apology and paid 'an acceptable sum' into court in settlement of the claim. He also paid Mr Greenwood's costs.

Mr Brewer was still not satisfied. In 1969 he called a public meeting to discuss a 'full documented history of over twenty planning decisions' for which he obtained details from the planning office.

A more serious allegation was made by a large nationally known developer in regard to the redevelopment of a former Newfoundland warehouse on the Quay. The business of H and A Burden and Company, sailmakers and ships' chandlers, was acquired in 1957 by the Cope, Allman group, whose managing director was Leonard Matchan, a former borough councillor. In 1959, Christopher Hill Ltd erected a new grain handling plant, 85 feet high, on the Quay. The building was a short distance from Burdens' premises, for which, within a few months, outline planning permission was granted for a seven-storey block of showrooms, flats and offices. Some eight years later, the truth of Alderman Miller's assertion that Planning Committees, and policies, could change from year to year, appeared to be borne out.

The site came on the market, and in 1968 a developer sought to take advantage of the 1960 planning permission. The committee was in a dilemma. It deferred its decision past the date when the developer could apply to the Minister to determine the new application. It had been received in the same year that Southern Gas Board dismantled its enormous coal gantry on the Quay, which was rapidly changing from a working quay to a recreational area. The committee was concerned that such a high building would affect the amenities of properties behind the Quay, which since 1960 had been transformed into a residential precinct from an area of poor housing, factories and warehouses.

The Times carried a full page advertisement from the developer complaining that the committee's procrastination and change of mind showed Poole's administration of planning control was inefficient and lax. It published a story listing the iniquities of the committee. It asserted that it settled planning decisions 'over a bottle of wine' and gave plans only a cursory look before approving them. It claimed that the officers had not

Alderman James Steptoe

advised the committee of the proximity of listed buildings, The story, suitably embellished, appeared in the columns of the satirical magazine *Private Eye*.

Committee members were shocked enough to appoint an independent panel of local architects to advise on difficult applications for planning approval. It was not long, however, before the architects suggested that as they had seen no reason to question the advice of the Borough Architect their intervention was unnecessary.

Perhaps it was not surprising that two such cases should occur among the 35,000 planning decisions made during the decade. With every planning decision affecting the value of land and the neighbouring amenities, a great strain fell on officers and members alike. Sometimes it could be too much, as in the case of a planning application for a cement depot. Even before the Committee had begun considering it, a 'Broadstone Fighting Fund' was established, to which, it was said, Poole's Member of Parliament had subscribed. It was also said that the MP had written to the Minister suggesting that if he took a careful look at the plan he might think the only option was to revoke or modify it,

This was too much for be overwrought Chairman, Alderman James Steptoe. He resigned his chairmanship, and announced: 'I have no longer any wish to accept the outside and sometimes unnecessary pressures the duties have brought upon me.' Political overtones bedevilled planning administration on some local issues, he said, and the impression had been given that there was a lack of faith in the ability of the Conservative council to manage its affairs. In the case in point, be added, the plan had not even been considered by his committee. Why then, he asked, was the Broadstone Fighting Fund raised? Who was fighting whom?

The Planning Committee had withstood many storms as it battled for years with its heavy work load. It was an unfortunate episode, especially as it came so shortly before the dissolution of the old Council.

The committee had many other duties, apart from planning control. They included preparing plans for the redevelopment of Old Poole; suggesting the line of the new lateral road and the site of the Towngate Bridge; and district plans for Merley, Bearwood, Creekmoor, Mannings Heath, Canford Heath and the waterfront, to say nothing of its policy of extending Tree Preservation Orders.

POOLE'S HEALTH

THE PERSONAL HEALTH AND WELFARE SERVICES

Dr James Hutton, Medical Officer of Health

The Personal Health and Welfare Services, administered by the Corporation, employed five doctors, some forty trained nurses and their supporting administration staff. It was an expensive service, and a vitally important one to most residents at some time in their life. It was a service that was generally not well known, and its origin and responsibility were not usually credited to the Corporation.

During the 1960s the service developed to meet the changing conditions of the town. The completion of the Maternity Wing of Poole Hospital, for instance, resulted in more and more births taking place in hospital, rather than in a mother's own home with the service of a midwife. In 1961 over 700 babies were delivered by the Corporation midwives. By 1965, the number had fallen to 409 and, by 1969, to 199. To cope with the growing number of births taking place in the hospital it adopted the practice of early discharge of mothers and babies, who were then cared for at home by midwives. It was a practice that would clearly become standard.

The duties of the District Nurses also changed. Some were attached to doctors' surgeries to act as medical auxiliaries where, for instance, they were qualified to give injections, change dressings, take blood pressure and similar tasks. Their duties at clinics were extended in 1957 to include family planning advice, including advice on contraception 'on social grounds.' In conjunction with the pathological department of the hospital, the nurses also offered a service of cervical cytology and did much to advocate the benefits of early diagnosis of cervical cancer. Although 700 attendances for this service were made in 1966, the response was considered disappointing and a public meeting was held to publicise the service.

The Health Visitors' duties remained much as before. They acted as school nurses, assisting the medical staff with their duties of regular inspection of school children and giving them their regular vaccination and immunisation injections. They also performed follow-up visits to children under five, expectant mothers, and problem families. It was a similar case with the Home Help Service. The eighty trained women not only helped where it was needed, because of illness or old age; they were often able to give early warning to the welfare services of other needs of members of a household.

Other services, such as the services to the elderly, had to be extended. By 1966 there were over 2,000 elderly people on the register of those needing some help. One of the aims of the service was to help people to live a happy and independent life in their own home. Domiciliary services were provided, such as the attendance of District Nurses. Luncheon and social clubs were formed, and a Day Centre was provided at Parkstone. 'Meals on wheels' were provided in co-operation with the WRVS, who delivered over 10,000 meals a year to some 200 elderly people. Some elderly people who needed readily available help were rehoused in specially built bungalows with warden service, which the Corporation's Housing Department provided in increasing numbers. Those who could not manage on their own, even with this amount of help, were taken into one of the elderly persons' homes.

There were, too, many classes of residents who required specialised help, such as the dumb, blind, the deaf and physically handicapped. In 1969 there were 340 blind and 50 partially blind residents, 40 deaf and 70 'hard-of hearing' and the numbers registered as handicapped and needing help had risen to nearly 400. They were visited by the welfare department which gave such help as it could. There were three social welfare officers responsible for helping the blind. Day classes were held at Belmont, the county council's blind home, social meetings were arranged, and some holidays provided for them. For the deaf a 'Hard-of-Hearing Club' was formed at the Poole Training Centre and, in conjunction with the Salisbury Diocesan Association, lip-reading classes were held. Two senior health visitors were appointed to help the disabled. They arranged for their homes to be adapted to improve their quality of life. In co-operation with the Red Cross, loans of aids, wheelchairs and the like were organised. The department also issued Disabled Drivers badges to facilitate the parking of cars driven by the disabled or in which they were passengers.

The intractable problem of the time was that of mental health. In 1964 there were 165 mentally disturbed or subnormal residents registered with the department. Social clubs were established to give some relief to parents or carers, and some patients were given practical work at the Poole Training Centre. By 1967, however, the numbers suffering from some mental illness had risen to 376, with 207 registered as mentally subnormal. These cases entailed 3,200 yearly home visits by the staff.

By 1966 the policy of discharging patients from Herrison Hospital to take up their lives in the community led to over 100 patients being discharged. In the short term, that did not reduce the work of the department for, in the same year, it was necessary to return 113 patients to hospital following a relapse, usually because they failed to continue medication after discharge.

Dorset County Council established a hostel for recuperating patients as well as supplying a home for the mentally infirm. The Hospital Board provided a day-hospital to give out-patient facilities, and the Corporation provided a large Training Centre in Plantation Road at which up to 100 adult trainees could receive training in practical skills. There were also school facilities for 80 children. The Centre was provided with a swimming pool and was staffed by a Manager, a Senior Supervisor and five supervisors. It was the largest in the south of England, and the department was proud of its achievements.

The centre was opened by Mrs Rene Montague at about the time Parliament passed the Local Authorities Social Services Act, 1970, which gave the Secretary of State the power to reorganise the welfare services. Poole Council felt that its record justified it being allowed to continue its work in this field. It claimed that its services had benefited from close integration with the housing, health and education services of the council, which might be lost if the service was to be administered by another authority, but it was to no avail. The Secretary of State transferred the powers to the county council in April 1971.

ENVIRONMENT CONTROL

The Public Health Department was also responsible for assuring that the environment of the town was conducive to its citizens' well-being. Its duties extended to almost everything needed to enable residents to enjoy a healthy existence, its scope ranging from the air people breathed, the food and water they consumed, their houses, and the places where they worked or took recreation, to the noise to which they were afflicted.

Six of the eight inspectors of health, under the supervision of the Medical Officer of Health and the Chief Inspector, had special responsibilities for particular areas of the town, as well as other general duties.

One of their duties was in the operation of the Clean Air Act, designed to restrict the amount of smoke and the emission of sulphur dioxide. Air was monitored at three main stations established in the town in 1964. Three quarters of air pollution in Poole in the early 1960s arose from domestic fires, and the amount of smoke in the Poole atmosphere decreased by 50% between 1964 and 1969. The main invisible pollutant in the atmosphere was sulphur dioxide, which tended to increase with the rising use of oil, especially heavy oil, in the increasing number of industrial premises. Special attention to this aspect achieved a considerable reduction in the levels of sulphur dioxide in the air.

The inspectors made regular visits to shops selling food, and to restaurants, hotels and boarding houses to ensure the safe handling of food. All the hotels of Poole co-operated with the department in a course of lectures given on the subject, and certificates were given to participants who satisfactorily completed it.

The bigger food chains were beginning to take their responsibilities for hygiene

The old gasworks was part of the street scene for many Old Town residents, but that did not deter the Council from seeking to create improvement areas.

very seriously and appointed their own inspectorate, usually recruited from local authority public health inspectors. When the managing director of Marks and Spencer stores was criticised for poaching inspectors, trained at authorities' expense, he remained unabashed. He said that it was the local authorities' fault for not paying them enough! Whatever precautions were taken by the larger food distributors, however, the need for inspection was hardly reduced. Contaminated food sold by them might well affect a great many more people than if it came from a small corner shop. The inspections were maintained, despite serious difficulty after 1970 in the recruitment of qualified staff.

One of the other important duties of the inspectors was to try to ensure that all houses were brought up to a minimum standard. In the early 1960s much of their time was taken up in inspecting every house in the slum clearance areas and making a very detailed report on its condition. After 1967 inspectors turned their attention to trying to ensure that all tenanted houses were brought up to habitable standards. By 1968 over three thousand houses had been inspected. In most cases the houses were brought up to the required standard voluntarily. Only a few owners had to be taken to court for a compulsory order to be made.

The inspectors could not then insist on owners improving their property by providing the 'standard amenities' of a bath, a wash basin with hot and cold water, an inside water closet and a food store, except by declaring an 'Improvement Area' under the 1964 Housing Act. It was a complicated procedure, little used by local authorities.

In 1968, Poole became the first authority in the south to declare improvement areas, covering some 100 houses in two areas of the borough. Once approved, they gave the Council power to insist on owners providing all the 'standard amenities' mentioned above. The Council demonstrated how a house in Emerson Road could be improved and provided with these amenities. This work cost £974 and attracted a grant of £800. Because of the cumbersome and prolonged procedure for declaring improvement areas, only two such orders were made before the passing of the Housing Act, 1969. This Act simplified the procedure designed to prolong the life of existing houses by ensuring that they contained the minimum standards of equipment and were put into a good state of repair.

The official government estimate was that, in 1969, four million houses in Britain, a quarter of the country's housing stock, did not reach this standard, but that the proportion in the south of the country was 13%. A survey of houses in Poole showed that the total that required repair or the addition of the 'standard amenities' was 1,670. This constituted 4.7% of Poole's houses, a figure that the health inspectors claimed was due in part to their earlier vigilance.

The inspectors' work also included the inspection of shops, offices, factories and workshops to ensure their sanitary condition, temperature control, lighting, accident control and washing facilities. Their powers regarding noise control, however, were then very limited. Though 'undesired sound' could be measured in decibels, whether it was a 'statutory nuisance' was a very subjective matter. At the same time, it was obvious that more noise was being generated as road traffic increased, the appetite grew for loud pop music, and more ventilation systems and machinery entered the workplace. Although more people complained of noise, the inspectors could do little more than persuade the perpetrators to abate the nuisance. At one time they suggested that the Health Committee should institute a month's publicity campaign under the slogan of 'Keep Poole Quiet'!

POOLE HOSPITAL

The building of the long-awaited Poole Hospital was finally completed in 1969 and the townspeople were delighted to hear that the Queen had agreed to come to Poole formally to declare the hospital open.

The weather in Poole on July 11, 1969, was sunny and warm, ideal for the visit of the Queen and Duke of Edinburgh. They arrived just after three o'clock, having driven into the town from Upton Road and Fleets roundabout. As the royal couple stepped out of their car they were greeted by a fanfare given by the trumpeters of the Royal Hussars. The Lord Lieutenant then introduced the Mayor, Alderman Arthur Lloyd-Allen who, in turn, introduced the civic party to the Queen and Duke.

They continued into the hospital where Philip Templeman, chairman of Wessex Regional Hospital Board, gave an address of welcome to which the Queen responded. Her Majesty unveiled a plaque to commemorate her visit and declared the hospital open. H Morgan Williams, chairman of the medical staff, gave an address of thanks, and the Bishop of Salisbury dedicated the hospital.

The Queen and Duke made a tour of five departments of the hospital, already occupied by patients, where she met the leading consultants and representatives of the staff. Tea was than served in the hospital library and four other locations in the hospital as music was provided by the bands of the Royal Armoured Corps and Royal Hussars.

Nursing staff provided a guard of honour as the reception party escorted the Queen and Duke out on to the forecourt of the hospital where their car was waiting. They drove through Poole Park, which was crowded with residents, children and holidaymakers, through Commercial Road to Pottery Junction, Ashley Road and Ringwood Road. There were crowds of people all along this route, who had a good view of the royal guests as they waved their greetings.

The Queen and Duke were in the town barely two hours, but made a lasting impression on the people they met and the thousands who waved to them as they passed.

The Mayor, Arthur Lloyd-Allen, introduces the Queen and Prince Philip to official guests at the opening of Poole General Hospital. They include the Town Clerk, the Recorder of Poole, Malcolm McGougan, and Mrs McGougan.

The new Poole General Hospital, with its multi-storey nurses' accommodation block in the foreground.

Top: Work in progress on Poole General Hospital.

Left: The Mayor invites the Queen to sign the visitors' book.

INDUSTRY

THE PORT OF POOLE

The conflicting interests in the harbour and port of Poole, particularly as regards the role of the Quay, came to a head in the last decade of the existence of 'the Town and County of Poole.' Although the board of Poole Harbour Commissioners had general responsibilities over the harbour as a whole, its principal concerns prior to 1968 had been the maintenance of the main channel and fostering the commercial uses of the Quay.

For centuries everyone living in Poole had been, directly or indirectly, dependent on the trade of the port. In the early 19th century, more than 90 per cent of the working population owed their livelihood to the sea or the harbour. By the mid-1960s, that proportion had declined to less than 20 per cent. Commander Nicholas Mules, the harbour board's doughty Clerk, Chief Executive and Collector of Dues, was eventually to admit that most people living outside the Old Town regarded Poole as a shopping, holiday and yachting centre. To Commander Mules, however, it was also a thriving and expanding commercial port, and he would not willingly yield an inch on the question of which interest should predominate on the Quay.

Traders had sometimes taken issue with the Commissioners as to how the business of the harbour should be regulated, but none had questioned the primacy of its business over any other uses of the harbour or the Quay.

By 1964, although 400,000 tons of cargo were unloaded from the 1,500 ships visiting the port, and nearly 100 dockers were still employed there, few Poole people had any interest in the trade of the port. On the other hand, nearly all of them had concern for the well-being of the harbour, even if it was only to enjoy the refreshing sight of some aspect of it from their homes or as they went about the town. Growing numbers, too, were 'messing about in boats' or sailing on the waters of the harbour.

The Quay, too, was becoming a favourite place for residents and visitors to witness the unloading of vessels, and the various visiting yachts; to take a drink in one of the public houses or merely enjoy the wide view across the harbour.

The Harbour Commissioners complained to the Council that their unloading areas were being obstructed and that stalls selling ice cream, soft drinks, whelks and cockles, which had followed the influx of people to the quayside, were impeding port traffic. The police agreed that stalls along the side of the road formed a dangerous

In Poole in the 1960s, the sun was setting on the vision of Town Quay as a working quayside where traditional cargoes were handled by stevedores. The Quay and its warehouses began to take on a new role as tourist attractions.

Top: The grain handling plant on Poole Quay. Bottom: Poole Quay.

The face of Miss World 1964 (Ann Sidney), and the body of a mermaid: the Poole coat of arms as depicted on the new Harbour Office in High Street, opened in 1966.

obstruction, and the Council brought a prosecution against the stall holders. The Magistrates ruled, however, that the Poole Corporation Act, which banned sales of any commodity within fifty feet of the seafront, did not apply to the quayside. It was only after the Corporation obtained further Parliamentary powers that the stalls were finally removed.

The Corporation's sympathy in the early 1960s was still with the Commissioners' view that the prime use of the Quay was commercial. In pursuance of this view, it had given planning permission for a grain handling plant on the quayside, and a large grain drying silo. It was convinced that both were necessary to maintain the business of the port. At the same time, it discouraged the intensification of public use of the Quay by refusing planning permission for an amusement arcade in one of the old warehouses.

The trade on the Quay still had some significance to the prosperity of the town, as was demonstrated as late as 1970 and 1972. In those years, when the dockers 'withdrew their labour,' it was reported that firms such as Christopher Hill, Yeatmans and Oakley Brothers had suffered significant losses. Ships were unable to unload, and had to wait at anchor outside the harbour entrance.

In November 1966, the Commissioners transferred their offices to a new premises at 4 High Street. They were erected on the site of the library presented to the town in 1833 by its Members of Parliament, Benjamin Lester Lester and the Hon W F Ponsonby. In its layout, the new building in many ways closely resembled the Georgian Harbour Office on the quayside. Built at a cost of £18,000, with a large boardroom as its central feature, the new Harbour Office was fitted out in a manner designed to reflect the best contemporary craftsmanship. The Poole coat of arms on the front of the building was surmounted by a mermaid with the face of Ann Sidney, the Poole beauty queen who became Miss World in 1964.

Whatever the resemblance between the old and new buildings, it was already obvious that the role of the port and its guardians was changing. In February 1966, the Conservative Bow Group had put forward proposals for the country's first national sea park, including the harbour, Poole Bay, and the western Solent. Pointing to the fact that some 500,000 people, mainly in the south-east of the country, were now actively involved in sailing, the report even proposed limiting commercial shipping in the Solent at some times of the year. In 1968, when the Government was considering reorganisation of small ports, Poole Council urged the need for *a unified and positive approach to yachting needs in Poole Harbour.* It claimed that although there were ten yacht clubs in the harbour, the Commissioners had done little to encourage the growth and development of yachting, apart from approving new moorings and byelaws. The Commissioners had already upset the local yachting fraternity in 1965, by levying dues on all pleasure craft 10 feet or more in length, while rejecting calls for direct representation for yachtsmen on the harbour board.

Between 1968 and 1972, the Commissioners claimed, trade in the port increased from 995,021 to 1,162,253 tonnes a year. Only a small proportion of this was handled by dockers, even though, in the same period, cargo handled by dockers rose from 100,414 to 166,731 tonnes. Most commercial users had their own wharves. Southern

Gas Board imported some 200,000 tons of coal a year at Gas Quay. Poole Generating station had a separate wharf, as did a number of timber and petroleum importers. The reduction in the general trade of the port was shown by the reduced number of dockers. Their numbers declined from 280 in 1939, to only 44 who took part in the 1972 strike.

Prior to 1968, the Commissioners were primarily responsible for conservancy of the harbour, but in that year, following reform of the National Dock Labour Scheme, they also became the port's sole employers of registered dock workers. The register was reduced to approximately 46 men, and casual piecework was abolished in favour of permanent employment for a regular workforce. This gave the Commissioners a more direct involvement in the fortunes of the commercial port. These, however, would soon come to rely even less on conventional cargoes handled by stevedores on Town Quay.

After 1970, with the dismantling of the huge gasworks coal gantry, which had blighted the recreational use of the quayside, the whole aspect of the Quay was changed. Pedestrians could then walk unobstructed from Poole Bridge all the way to Fishermen's Dock, and the Corporation began to change its view on the use of the quayside. Despite the Commissioners' complaint that lack of space was strangling harbour trade, and despite unresolved arguments as to the ownership of the land from which the railway lines had been removed, the Corporation established a small car park on the Quay. When a man and a woman were drowned in a car which fell over the quayside, it was suggested that the Commissioners should erect bollards along the Quay

Fishermen's Dock, with the Gasworks coal gantry in the background.

frontage to obviate this danger. The Commissioners refused, and reminded the public that the Quay was *a working quay, not a promenade*.

By then, the Commissioners were slowly losing the battle. The Minister overruled the Corporation's refusal to permit an amusement arcade on the Quay. The Corporation gave planning permission for a row of permanent kiosks to be built on the corner of the Quay and Lagland Street, to accommodate some of the stallholders displaced from the quayside. It also bought land facing the Quay that was not required by the Gas Board after demolition of the coal gantry. The Corporation considered that this site, facing directly up the line of the main channel of the harbour, would be ideal for a hotel. Many hotels in the town had been demolished to become sites for housing and flat development. The Harbour Commissioners objected strongly to such a use. They complained that the land was needed for commercial uses ancillary to the port, such as warehouses or bulk cargo handling.

Commander Mules realised that conditions had changed on the Quay. Looking through the town's old Acts of Parliament, he found one passed in the early nineteenth century, which gave statutory powers to the Corporation, as Commissioners of the harbour, to reclaim land at Hamworthy. He asked the Town Clerk whether these powers had passed to the present Harbour Board.

It was the beginning of the mass transfer of the Commissioners' business away from the Quay to the Hamworthy side of the port. In 1971 the Commissioners agreed

An early Truckline ferry.

a three-stage plan to accomplish this. Stage 1 was to reclaim six and a half acres of land west of New Quay; Stage 2 was to reclaim a further four acres westward to accommodate a roll-on, roll-off ferry; and Stage 3 was to build quays round the reclamation to develop cargo handling facilities.

In 1972 the Ministry lent the Commissioners £565,000, to build a new ferry terminal. In June 1973, a roll-on, roll-off ferry was inaugurated by Truckline, an Anglo-French company. Their service, for freight vehicles only, sailed from Poole at 8pm to arrive at Cherbourg at 4am, leaving Cherbourg again at 2 pm to return to Poole at 7pm. It was an immediate success, thanks largely to the policy that no private cars with passengers could use it, and special arrangements on both sides of the Channel for rapid clearance by the port authorities. In 1974, Truckline secured contracts for the import of 2,000 French tractors in a two-year period, and of up to 25,000 Citroen cars a year. Within 18 months of operation, traffic on Truckline ferries had grown to 1,500 vehicle movements a month.

The transformation of the use of the Quay was by then almost complete.

ACT OF PARLIAMENT

Poole Corporation had promoted four Acts of Parliament since 1847. The first was in 1919, and mainly related to the purchase of Poole Bridge from Lord Wimborne. The second in 1927 was to obtain power to operate a bus service. The third, in 1937, was to give the Corporation general powers, including more in relation to the Bridge. The 1961 Act gave the Corporation powers to regulate trading on the Quay and to amend the restrictive covenants on Sandbanks recreation ground.

In 1964, the large increase in the numbers of yachts needing Poole Bridge to be lifted created serious congestion of road traffic on both sides of the bridge. The Corporation decided that the provision in the original Act of Parliament, which insisted on the bridge being raised on demand by any vessel wishing to pass, must be modified. At the same time, it was essential to remove the turbary rights attached to six pieces of land owned by the Corporation to allow their development.

Before the Town Clerk's staff drafted the proposed Act, other departments of the Corporation were asked if there were other powers which they needed to facilitate their work. The final draft of the Bill, which was deposited with Parliament for its 1964/5 session, contained 58 sections and two schedules.

The two meetings of the Council, required by statute, were held in November, 1964, and in January, 1965, after a public meeting of local government electors approved the Bill. After meetings with the officers of the Ministry of Housing and Local Government, and those of the Ministries of Transport and Health, the Bill came before the House of Lords in February 1965. The House of Lords passed it for scrutiny by Lord Chairman of Committees and his colleagues. They heard evidence from the Corporation's witnesses and representatives from the various Ministries.

The Bill survived the scrutiny of the House of Lords' Committee intact, apart from two sections which the Ministry of Housing and Local Government opposed. It was then passed back to the House of Lords where it passed both readings in the House. After that it was passed as an uncontested Bill to the House of Commons where it again had to survive its two readings.

The final reading of the Bill took place in the Commons in April 1965. It received Royal Assent that autumn, to become the Poole Corporation Act, 1965.

INDUSTRY

The Poole Plan in 1960, showing how the Corporation should encourage the town's future development, proposed to reserve a considerable area of land for new industrial premises. The Government, however, disagreed. Its policy was to encourage new industry in the north of the country, where unemployment was higher, and it would need a very strong case to grant an industrial development certificate in Poole. It therefore radically reduced this allocation.

This decision was one the Corporation considered unfavourable to the town's interests. From 1960 onwards there had been a great influx of people. The 1966 sample census showed that 17,700 people had moved into Poole between 1961 and 1965. There had also been a considerable exodus of younger people from the town in search of

Although more modern methods of gas-making were introduced during the decade, the buildings of Poole Gasworks continued to overshadow much of the Old Town.

employment. With the proportion of retired people approaching the 29% of Bournemouth, it was important to achieve a better balance by encouraging more job opportunities in the town. There were also serious financial reasons. Poole's rates were consistently half as high again as Bournemouth's. Three-quarters of the rate burden in Poole fell on residential properties, whereas Bournemouth enjoyed a large contribution from shops and hotels. With the loss of hotels in Poole to other forms of development, such as flats, the proportion of the rates paid by hoteliers, which had been approaching three per cent before the second world war, had fallen by half, and could hardly be hoped to increase greatly. It was therefore only rate income from new industry, offices and shops that could redress the balance and bring Poole more into line with its neighbour to the east.

One way in which new enterprise could be encouraged was to promote Poole as an attractive place in which to live and work. This approach succeeded when Barclays Bank DCO was considering which of 16 towns it should choose for its relocation away from London. Similarly, when the Bolton Group of companies moved to Poole, the facilities of the town and the proximity of the new hospital were instrumental in the decision.

It was equally important to retain and encourage the expansion of existing businesses. With Britain's entry into the Common Market, it was thought that only the largest exporters would be able to thrive, and larger firms began to take over local companies. In this way, many Poole firms became subsidiaries of larger companies based elsewhere.

Some that were taken over, such as Hamworthy Engineering (taken over by Powell Duffryn), Wallis Tin (Metal Box), Christopher Hill (Ranks, Hovis McDougall) Wykes Engineering (Taylor Woodrow), gained from the added strength of their new parents. Others, such as the Sharp, Jones pottery at Branksome, taken over by Redland Holdings; Bluebird Caravans (Caravans International); or Humphris Engineering, eventually ceased production in Poole. Some old-established Poole companies also passed out of existence, among them South-Western Pottery at Parkstone, whose land became a new housing estate, and Oakley Brothers, established on the Quay for 160 years, which was originally founded to provide salt to preserve the cod caught by Poole's fishing fleet.

There were notable gains to Poole's employment opportunities. Nuclear Graphite took over the old Royal Ordnance Factory in Sopers Lane. The Plessey Company later took over the premises, a development thought to be of such importance that the Mayor had to delay informing a Council meeting until after the close of business on the Stock Exchange. Once installed in Sopers Lane, Plessey's newly formed automation division set out a much-vaunted programme of expansion, which in the end was only partly implemented. Loewy Engineering and British Drug Houses, which had come to Poole during the war, continued to prosper. Loewy built new premises in Wallisdown Road and BDH built a large warehouse and offices in Broom Road, Parkstone.

In 1964, twelve new factories were built and 20 extended. In 1966, 42,800 people of Poole were in employment. By 1971 this total had risen to 47,585. Against this background, in 1968, Alderman Fred Rowe sponsored the setting up of Wessex Export

Top: Hamworthy Engineering's factory at Fleetsbridge.
Bottom: The factory of Hydromation Engineering at Hamworthy, which manufactured machine tool cleaning and filtration equipment for the motor industry. The company expanded rapidly after moving to Poole and by 1965 had 130 employees.

The new Plessey factory at Waterloo.

Closer ties developed between industry and local government as Poole expanded. Here the Town Clerk and the Borough Engineer, Robert Hawker (centre) are in discussion with Douglas Smith (left), of Hamworthy Engineering.

Poole Generating Station.

Club, with Joshua Seiger as Chairman, to help firms in the region to export their goods. It became an influential body in the commercial life of the area, even mounting a delegation that was well received by the government of South Africa.

In 1969, Poole industrialists, with the help of Dorset County Council, as the authority responsible for further education, formed an Industrial Training Unit. Its premises were in the grounds of Poole Technical College. The first of three Poole Trades and Industry Fairs was staged on Ladies' Walking Field in 1965. Further ones were held at the Stadium car park and Whitecliff Recreation Ground. Some observers considered Poole's wave of prosperity was the biggest since the Newfoundland trade. The town had also been able to attract considerable office development: Unlike Bournemouth, it lay just outside a region to which Government restrictions on office deveopment applied. Orchard House, an office block in High Street, was built on a site provided by the Corporation in return for the developers building a public multi-storey car park. The national headquarters of the Royal National Lifeboat Institution was built on land vacated by St Mary's Roman Catholic Church, which built a new church on land acquired from the Corporation in Wimborne Road. The Frizzell Group built a modern office block on the island site at County Gates.

Between 1970 and 1972, 41 firms employing at least ten people moved to Poole, including Barclays, Bolton Group, Brocks Group, Wigmore Bindery, RNLI and Norman Frizzell. The *Property Investment Review* wrote that 'while many towns could offer good environment and labour resources within 90 minutes travelling time from London, all don't have go-ahead councils, a cohesive town, and sea, sun, heath and forest as Poole does.'

The Nuffield industrial estate.

NUFFIELD ESTATE

The Corporation did more than merely encourage business and seek to facilitate planning approvals. It had often been able to provide land for development. The owner of land over which Fleets Lane had been extended sold land to the north to the Corporation for a new housing estate. She then asked it to buy the rest of her land, to the south of the new road. Her ownership extended to the borders of Holes Bay, over which the Corporation planned a new main road to the west. After making provision for the road, an area of low lying land was left which, when later the railway line to Creekmoor, Broadstone and Wimborne was discontinued, left a considerable area for industrial development. The Corporation built a road to serve this area, with access from Fleets Lane at two points. One or two sites were sold for development before 1974, when the land, having been purchased under the Road Traffic Acts, was transferred to the County Council.

The Corporation also obtained approval for a loan to buy 53 acres of land off Old Wareham Road for an industrial estate. It argued that it needed sites to offer firms affected by redevelopment proposals, particularly in the Old Town, and that four such firms were willing to move if a suitable site could be found. There were also firms that the Corporation wished to move out of residential areas, four of which had agreed to

How it turned out: a more recent aerial photograph showing the Hamworthy Engineering factory in Waterloo Road, with the Nuffield industrial estate and Canford Heath housing development beyond; and, in the foreground, the enlarged sewage treatment works and the Fleetsbridge intersection.

accept a Discontinuation of Use Order as soon as they had an alternative site.

The land for the Nuffield industrial estate was purchased in early 1965, but because of restrictions on capital expenditure, it was the end of 1966 before roads and services could be provided. After allowing for an adjustment of boundaries with Hamworthy Engineering and Marley Tiles, and for the area required for roads, there were 44 acres of land costing an average of just over £9,000 an acre.

Despite national economic difficulties, there were many applications for sites on the new estate, and 18 of them were sold or let in 1966. In April 1967, the Borough Treasurer reported that the outstanding loan on the development was costing £5,440 a year, which was more than offset by rent income of £15,440. By the following year 45 firms were operating in the estate.

It was then showing a healthy profit as well as clearly fulfilling all the Corporation's hopes. In 1972, the estate was extended.

Top: Civic services and church parades were an important part of the Council's year.

Left: Alderman Fred Rowe

TOWN AFFAIRS
SOCIAL ACTIVITIES

During the 1960s there were many social activities to which representatives of the Council and its officers were invited. The main trade, social and sporting organisations of the town would hold an annual dinner and dance at which it was the custom for the Mayor to be asked to respond to the toast to *The Borough and County of the Town of Poole*.

On these occasions, it was fair game for the chairman of the organisation to include some criticism of the Council, but it was always given and taken in good humour. There was, however, one striking exception. At the annual dinner and dance of the Poole, Bournemouth and District Chamber of Commerce at the Savoy Hotel, Bournemouth, in 1967, John Cordle, MP for Bournemouth West, criticised nationalisation and the building of schools, hospitals and housing with money 'squandered by Wilson and his gang.' This was too much for Ron Hart, the Labour Mayor of Poole, who took great exception, remarking that the speech 'had turned the meal sour in his stomach!'

Every six weeks there was a Council meeting at which the Mayor presided. Every quarter there was a Quarter Sessions court at which the Sheriff sat with the Recorder. On the first day of the Sessions the Sheriff gave a luncheon in the Municipal Buildings to the Recorder and the barristers and officials attending the court. The newly elected Mayor and Sheriff attended the annual Civic Service, usually in St James' Parish Church, but sometimes in the Mayor's place of worship. The annual Service of Remembrance at St James' was also attended by members of the council and its officers, together with representatives of the armed forces and the civilian support services. It was also the practice of the Mayor and Sheriff and their spouses to spend almost the whole of Christmas Day touring the wards of the hospitals, the almshouses and retirement homes.

The annual Mayor's Reception was the most important social event of his year of office. It was one at which he could show the Council's appreciation of the work of the town's leading industrialists, voluntary and charitable organisations, as well as reciprocate the invitations they had made to its civic leaders.

The event was usually held in the Municipal Buildings, which needed considerable temporary alterations to cater for between 500 and 700 guests. Large quantities of flowers and foliage were provided by the Parks Department; the Conference Room and Council Chamber were transformed for the occasion; and the inquiry offices of the Planning Department and Borough Treasurer were pressed into service as cloakrooms. Even so, it was necessary to erect a large marquee in the car park at the rear of the buildings.

The event inevitably caused some disruption to the everyday business of the Council offices, especially as the Council allowed NALGO, the officers' trade union, to use the same facilities the following evening. On the evening after that, the Council's manual staff enjoyed the same rights when they held what became known as the 'Workmen's Ball.' During these days the unsuspecting visitor was surprised to be faced with an entrance hall resembling a Kew greenhouse!

When Alderman Fred Rowe was Mayor in 1967-68, he felt that these facilities did not match the new standing of the town. He suggested that his many guests should be accommodated in a grander manner. Having obtained the Council's approval to erect a marquee in Poole Park, he hired what was said to be the largest one in Europe. When erected, the giant marquee extended along almost the entire frontage of the salt water lake, between Kingland Road and the boat compound. Electricity, main drainage and a water supply were laid on. Ernest Gale and the Parks Department excelled themselves in providing huge and exotic floral displays. In front of one of these the Mayor and Mayoress received their many guests, who included all members of Bournemouth Borough Council - as well as anyone who had agreed to contribute £10 to the Poole Sports Centre appeal!

No expense was spared. Des O'Connor was imported from a Bournemouth show for the cabaret. Music was provided by a steel band and a ballroom orchestra, and there was a lavish buffet.

Even on this occasion, one or two of Poole's inveterate complainers could find something to cavil at. One counted the number of journeys a Parks Department van had made between the marquee and the nurseries adjoining the park. He then complained to the District Auditor that not all these journeys had been charged to the Mayor's expenses. It was also claimed that the Council had not taken the proper steps to close part of the park to the public, and that access had not been maintained through the marquee for those ordinary citizens who might wish to walk among such scenes of civic splendour.

The Mayor had earlier announced that the evening's entertainment would end with a firework display. A dramatic setting had been chosen on the far side of the lake, adjoining the railway embankment. Unfortunately, as the festivities were ending, it started to rain, and most guests were unable to enjoy the full effect of the spectacle as, in their evening finery, they scrambled for shelter. The effect was not lost on the residents of homes near or overlooking the park, who had apparently gone to bed unaware of the impending display. As the set pieces were fading the whole harbour was lit up by cascading lights and the powerful explosions of rockets. Some residents reached for their telephones. One or two called the lifeboat station, believing a ship was in distress. One even feared an invasion had begun!

Miss World 1964, Ann Sidney of Parkstone, received a tremendous welcome from the people of Poole. The Mayor, Alderman Tom Sherrin, accompanied her on a triumphal drive from the town centre to the Municipal Buildings, where a civic banquet was given in her honour.

In 1964, when Ann Sidney of Parkstone, a former pupil of Kemp-Welch School, was chosen as Miss World, Tom Sherrin, the Mayor, felt the people of Poole would like to join in celebrating her success. He borrowed an open white Rolls-Royce in which he met Ann Sidney at Poole station on her return home, and took her on a triumphant tour of the town. In the evening he showed her off to the crowd that gathered outside the Municipal Buildings, where she was guest of honour at a civic dinner given by the Council.

This was the last straw for Councillor Geoffrey Adams, who thereupon resigned his seat on the Council. He maintained that it had illegally spent £253 on these events, and the costs should be charged to the members and officers who permitted it. He quoted the Corporation's standing orders, which forbade any expenditure not specifically provided for in the annual estimates, or previously agreed by the Finance Committee and the Council. The loss of Councillor Adams to the Council was a considerable one. He would not agree that on such exceptional occasions, it was reasonable to incur expenses in the hope that the Council would endorse them later.

In July, 1968, the Mayor, Mayoress, Sheriff and his wife and the Town Clerk attended a celebration of the work of Thomas Hardy in Westminster Abbey, to mark the fortieth anniversary of his death. Owing to wartime restrictions in 1940 there had been no commemoration of the centenary of his birth. It was a moving ceremony,

William Knapp   *Alderman Jack Mears*

starting with readings from *Tess of the D'Urbervilles, Under the Greenwood Tree* and *The Darkling Thrush*, followed by the Casterbridge Singers in a setting of *Afterwards*. The Rt. Hon. Harold Macmillan, the Festival President, placed flowers from Dorset on the memorial stone; Cecil Day Lewis, the Poet Laureate, read his *Birthday Poem for Thomas Hardy*, and the words of a poem by Charles I were sung, which ended

Then close thine eyes in peace and sleep secure,
no sleep so sweet as thine, no rest so sure.

In October 1968 Bob Hann, the Mayor, with the Sheriff and members of the Council and their wives, attended a festival of remembrance for the life and works of William Knapp (1698-1768), held at St James' Church and sponsored by the Society of Poole Men. William Knapp had served the church in a number of capacities, but it was as a composer of church music that he was famous. Many of his hymns were based on psalms and he had dedicated many of his tunes to Dorset towns.

At the festival, hymns with tunes dedicated to Canford and Wimborne, and his most famous hymn tune, *Wareham*, were sung by the combined choirs of Poole schools and churches, accompanied by the schools' orchestra and the church organ.

Towards the end of the celebration a hymn was sung to *Poole New Tune*, the words of which were most appropriate to the Poole of his day, and which began

They that in ships with courage bold
o'er swelling waves their trade pursue...

A civic dinner was among the celebrations to mark the four hundredth anniversary of the Charter of Elizabeth I.

A commemorative medal presented by the Sheriff of Southampton at celebrations to mark the 400th anniversary of the Charter of Elizabeth I.

In November the same year the Corporation celebrated the 400th anniversary of the town's principal charter, granted in 1568 by Elizabeth I. Eleven sheriffs from other towns [Bristol, Norwich, Lincoln, Southampton, Gloucester, Chester, Exeter, Lichfield, Worcester, Haverfordwest and Carmarthen] were invited to join in the celebrations. On Saturday, November 10, they attended a cocktail party given by Alderman Fred Rowe at the Municipal Buildings, where the borough's charters and civic regalia were displayed. The visiting sheriffs, together with the Chief Constable of Dorset and Bournemouth Constabulary and the Governor of HM Prison, Dorchester, attended a civic dinner at the Haven Hotel, Sandbanks. The Lord Lieutenant of Dorset (Colonel J W Weld) proposed the loyal toast, and the Sheriff of Bristol proposed a toast to Poole, to which Jack Mears, the Sheriff of Poole, replied. Bob Hann, the Mayor, proposed a toast to the visitors, to which the Sheriff of Norwich replied.

The following day, after a ceremonial procession from the Guildhall, the guests attended a Charter Service at St James' parish church. The congregation also included a number of former Sheriffs of Poole, county councillors, magistrates, Harbour Commissioners and Corporation officials.

In 1970 the Mayor and Sheriff took a full part in welcoming the Town Clerks of England when they chose Poole as the venue for their annual conference. Even though the Government had, immediately before the conference, announced a General Election, for which Town Clerks had special responsibilities, some 170 Town Clerks attended, taking over the Branksome Tower Hotel as headquarters. As if to signify the strict non-political stance of his calling, the Town Clerk of Bedford declared: 'Whatever the colour of their rosettes, a plague on all their houses if they erase the basic principles of local government!'

The year 1971 was notable for the granting of the Freedom of the Borough to two of the Council's members. It was the first time the honour had been bestowed since Sir Winston Churchill was made a Freeman in 1953. Alderman Arthur Lloyd-Allen had long been the unofficial leader of the Council. As an accountant and Chairman of the Finance and Redevelopment Committees, he kept a tight rein on the council's finances, but at the same time, sponsored major developments such as the Arndale shopping centre. Alderman Mrs Elsie Hickinson had given the Council the benefit of her clear and common sense opinions for 25 years, latterly as chairman of the Libraries Committee, which had improved its service greatly, as well as achieving a new central library. Both new Freemen had served as Sheriff and Mayor and on the Magistrates' Bench.

On June 9, 1971 the Council, in full regalia, processed from St James' Church through Thames Street and High Street to Scaplen's Court, where it unanimously resolved to offer the Freedom to these two members. Roy Holland, managing director of Poole Pottery, presented the Council with one of the 25 special plaques which Poole Pottery had made to celebrate the event.

Arthur Lloyd-Allen and Mrs Elsie Hickinson signing the Roll of Honorary Freemen of Poole.

The next day began a week's festival of events to celebrate the 600th anniversary of the Montacute Charter, which had first bestowed the title of 'Mayor' upon the town's leading citizen.

Arrangements for these events began the previous year when James Steptoe, Mayor in 1970, convened a meeting of 29 representatives of local organisations and businesses, who agreed to support a series of events to celebrate the anniversary, and appoint Joshua Sieger as chairman of the organising committee.

Celebrations began on June 10, 1971 with a morning service in St Osmund's Church, Parkstone, at which Adrian Greenwood, the Mayor, was a churchwarden. Afterwards, there was to be a display of dancing by children in Poole Park, followed by a 'Pirate Spectacular,' and a concert by the 70 members of the Junior Leaders Regimental Band. That evening the Mayor would switch on a floodlighting system for the park, intended as a permanent feature to mark the anniversary of the charter. During rehearsals for the historic moment, the lighting proved to be a great success. Bushes and borders took on superb shades, as the lights gave the park a most welcoming and almost fairyland effect.

The weather had been fine and sunny for the Council's meeting at Scaplen's Court the previous day, but it had only limited respect for these historic events. June 10, 1971 dawned to heavy rain, which continued unabated throughout the day. The luncheon in Compton Acres Gardens arranged by Mr John Brady was moved under canvas. Even there, rain managed to drip through on to the instruments of the Royal Marines band that played for the occasion.

The rest of the first day's programme had to be abandoned. It had been planned to have an ox-roasting ceremony in the park, at which slices of beef, placed in a bread roll, would be available all day at a cost of 15p. The ox-roasters gamely set up their spit and lit the fire, but were forced abandon their efforts. The ox was transported to Uddens slaughterhouse, the only cold store large enough to accommodate it. Later, when it was hoped to reinstate the ox-roast, sanitary inspectors condemned the whole carcass as unfit for human consumption.

However, the weather did not affect the evening's 'Medieval Feast' at Poole Technical College. Guests were asked to dress in medieval costume. Special arrangements were made with a firm in Bristol to hire appropriate costumes for the night. The Mayor, Adrian Greenwood, and the Lord of the Feast, Joshua Sieger, both arrived suitably costumed, but the Mayor was in his official car, and Mr Sieger in his inevitable Cadillac. Fred Rowe arrived, perhaps more appropriately, but more precariously, riding a large white horse, dressed as a knight, but inappropriately smoking a large Churchillian cigar.

The feast opened with a grace, *Non Nobis Domine* written in the 15th century, followed by a fanfare of trumpets as peacock and boar's head, salpicon of pheasant, lamb's tongue and mushroom, and other olden delicacies, were borne in.

Music provided by students of the College, and dance by pupils of Canford School of Dancing, accompanied the proceedings. At the end of the main meal, the diners were told to clean their platters, which had been specially designed by Poole Pottery, with their spicy rye bread. The meal was completed with *whipt syllabub, Pilcaithly*

Bannock, flummery coffins and divers fruits and subtleties.

The Queen's health was proposed by the Lord of the Feast. Lord Shackleton proposed the health of the town, to which Adrian Greenwood, the Mayor, replied. The proceedings were ended by the trumpeters with the old fanfare, composed about 1250, *Alle, psallite cum laya.*

In early 1972, Prince Charles, sailing in *HMS Scimitar* from Plymouth to Portsmouth, came into Poole with two companions to have dinner at the Antelope Hotel. After crab cocktail and Dover sole, they had drinks in the bar. The hosts, Charles and Mary Dowland, said regular customers showed 'only polite interest' in their visitor.

Many social activities of the Council involved the Royal Marines and their establishment at Hamworthy. One exploit by the Special Boat Section was specially honoured. It began with the New York harbour authority signalling to the liner *Queen Elizabeth 2* in mid-Atlantic that it believed a bomb had been placed on board. The

Left: Lieut–General Sir Ian Gourlay.
Below: Royal Marines march through the town centre as they celebrate the grant of the Freedom of Poole to their Corps.

liner had no personnel trained in detecting and disposing of bombs, and was more than two days' sailing from any port.

It was decided that the only quick way to get an expert bomb disposal squad on board was to parachute them into the sea, and for the ship's lifeboats to pick them up. These experts, however, were not experienced parachutists, let alone able to swim with their equipment in Atlantic waves and swell. In these desperate conditions, it was decided that members of the Special Boat Section, based at Poole, would carry the equipment and take responsibility for the safety of the bomb squad, parachuting with them into the sea. This heroic operation deserved a resounding finale, but it was not to be. No bomb was found on board. The New York harbour authority had been hoaxed.

By coincidence, Fred and Bertha Rowe were among the passengers on board the liner. Passengers had not been informed of the threat, and the first they heard of it was on a BBC news bulletin.

Most of the passengers had witnessed the courageous exploits of the Royal Marines and the bomb experts and they held a collection to show their admiration. Fred Rowe felt that this was insufficient recognition. He arranged for a reception at the Municipal Buildings in honour of the Royal Marines and members of the Special Boat Section involved.

The Mayor and Sheriff inspect the Royal Marines guard of honour during the freedom ceremony.

In March 1973, the Council resolved to offer the Corps of Royal Marines the Honorary Freedom of the Borough, 'to foster the existing mutual affection between the Corps and the citizens of Poole.' The formal ceremony was held on September 5 that year in Poole Park, when Lieut.-General Sir Ian Gourlay, Commandant-General, Royal Marines, received the Freedom on behalf of the Corps.

Four companies of Royal Marines, under the command of Lieut.-Colonel Sidwell, formed up in Poole Park opposite the cricket grandstand, at which the formalities of acceptance of the Freedom were completed. After speeches by Poole's two most recent Freemen, Aldermen Lloyd-Allen and Mrs Hickinson, the Mayor, Mrs Rene Montague, formally inspected the Royal Marine companies.

At a civic lunch in the Municipal Buildings Mrs Montague presented the Corps with a commemorative silver candelabrum, the candlestick supported by a depiction of a dolphin. The Royal Marines presented the town with a silver salver that depicted Marines leaping out of a landing craft.

Sir Ian Gourlay, in his speech, thanked the town for giving the Corps the highest honour it could bestow. This unsolicited gift, he declared, 'would symbolise the link between the citizens of Poole who wore plain clothes and the citizens of Poole who wear uniforms.'

During the evening the Royal Marines beat retreat in Poole Park under floodlights, and on the following Saturday 50 Royal Marine craft sailed past the Mayor, who took the salute from the Quay. Afterwards the Marines gave a display of their equipment and training methods, including abseil landing from helicopters and an exhibition of free-fall parachuting. It was a glorious day, with brilliantly coloured smoke trails from the falling parachutes seen against a clear blue sky. The ceremonies were concluded by the Corps exercising its newly acquired right as Freemen to parade with its band through the streets of Poole.

THE NEW COURTS

When the Municipal Buildings were erected in 1932, the Borough Council always intended to build a town hall and a central library on the civic centre site, as well as a swimming bath and courts buildings. Despite the Government promising money from the Unemployment Grants Committee toward the cost of the town hall, the cash-strapped Council of the day lost its courage and building did not continue.

By the 1950s, circumstances had changed. The Libraries and Parks Committees no longer believed that the civic centre was an appropriate site for a central library or a public swimming baths. The Council sold some of its land to the Government for the erection of the Crown Offices in Park Road. The site next to the police station in Sandbanks Road was earmarked for a courthouse to accommodate the Magistrates' Courts, the Court of Quarter Sessions and the County Court.

For the past 36 years all these courts had been accommodated in the Council Chamber or the Conference Room of the Municipal Buildings. With the growth of the town and the business of the courts, it had become increasingly difficult, sometimes

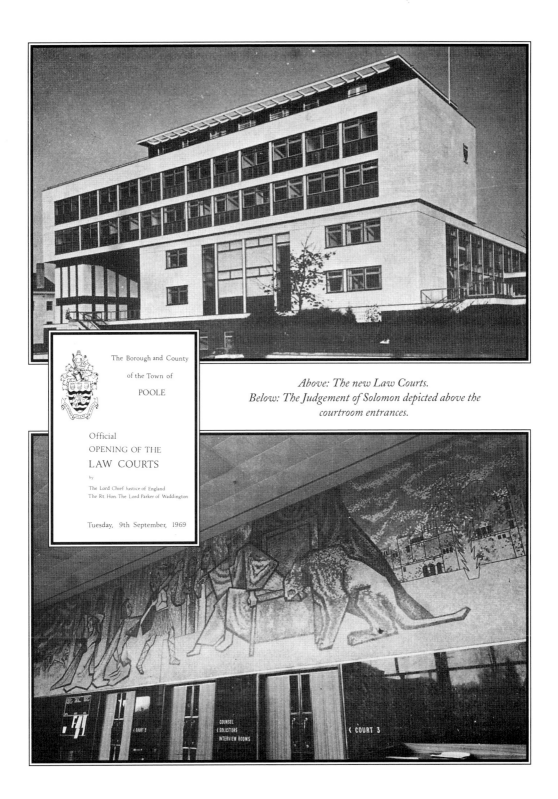

The Borough and County
of the Town of
POOLE

Official
OPENING OF THE
LAW COURTS
by
The Lord Chief Justice of England
The Rt. Hon. The Lord Parker of Waddington

Tuesday, 9th September, 1969

Above: The new Law Courts.
Below: The Judgement of Solomon depicted above the
courtroom entrances.

impossible, to accommodate all the sittings requested, for the rooms were also required for council meetings, public inquiries and town planning appeals. In 1960 the harassed Council began to press the Home Office for approval to build new courts. Plans were finally agreed in 1967.

The new building, designed by Geoffrey Hopkinson, the Borough Architect, with Don Hills as project architect, provided two Magistrates' Courts, one dual-purpose court for Quarter Sessions and the County Court, and a Juvenile Court. It also provided accommodation for the staff of the Magistrates' Court, the Probation Officers and the County Court. The building was completed in 1969, and officially opened in September that year by the Lord Chief Justice (Lord Parker). The ceremony was attended by the Mayor, Arthur Lloyd-Allen; the Member of Parliament and the chief officers of the police and the various courts. The Lord Chief Justice officially unveiled a plaque commemorating the event, and guests were taken a tour of the building. After a luncheon at the Royal Motor Yacht Club, the Lord Chief Justice gave an address in the Municipal Buildings to the magistrates of Poole, Bournemouth and Dorset .

COURT OF QUARTER SESSIONS

The Recorder of Poole ranked second only to the Mayor in the hierarchy of Poole citizens and, as such, often took his place with the Mayor on important civic occasions. The Court of Quarter Sessions, over which he presided, tried the more serious criminal

Presentation to Malcolm McGougan on his retirement as the last Recorder of Poole: The Town Clerk and Clerk of the Peace (John Hillier), the Sheriff (Denis Gooding), the Mayor (Adrian Greenwood), Mr McGougan and Judge David Pennant.

cases occurring in the borough, and heard appeals against decisions of the Magistrates. The court had, therefore, formed an important part in the life of the town since it was established under the Charter of Elizabeth I in 1568.

However, in the sweeping changes that the Government was making to local administration in the 1970s, the Court of Quarter Sessions was an early casualty. From January 1, 1972, the jurisdiction of the court was transferred to the Crown Court, and the offices of Recorder and Clerk of the Peace were abolished.

Since the Charter of Elizabeth I that established the court, thirty-two distinguished lawyers had served Poole as Recorder. It was ironic that the court and its juries, which had suffered for centuries from inconvenient accommodation, should attain a purpose-built court only within a year or two of its abolition: but there was no appeal from Parliament's decision.

The Council considered that this final chapter in the history of Poole Quarter Sessions should be marked by a civic dinner, and the occasion be taken to thank Malcolm McGougan, who had voluntarily served as Recorder since 1954. The dinner was held at the Branksome Tower Hotel in November, 1971. Adrian Greenwood, the Mayor, thanked Mr McGougan for his long service to the town and presented him with a pair of silver salvers to commemorate his service.

Judge David Pennant, the County Court Judge who was to take over the duties of the Quarter Sessions in the new Crown Court, clearly felt no great enthusiasm for the change. In his speech at the dinner he said *'Never has any elected Pope been more reluctantly dragged towards the chair of office. I can only think that it was all part of a great plan to relieve unemployment in the paper industry!'*

RECORDERS OF THE BOROUGH AND COUNTY OF THE TOWN OF POOLE SINCE THE GRANT OF THE CHARTER OF ELIZABETH I, 1568

1568	Giles Escourt	1846	William Hodges
1592	(circa) Richard Swayne	1857	William Major Cooke
1636	Ellis Swayne	1860	James Stephen
1639	William Constantyne	1864	Henry Bullar
1643-50	Vacancy - Recorder disqualified for suspected plot against the town of Poole	1870	John Francis Collier
		1873	Arthur John Hammond Collins
1650	Samuel Bond	1879	Gabriel Prior Goldney
1660	William Constantyne	1882	Henry Mason Bompas
1662	Anthony Ettricke	1885	George Pitt Lewis
1682	William Whyte	1904	Arthur Clavell Salter
1699	Nathaniel Bond	1917	Rayner Goddard
1707	Robert Erle	1924	William Thomas Lawrance
1719	Dennis Bond	1928	Harry Geen
1746	The Hon. James West	1939	Francis Seward Laskey
1772	John Bond	1941	Henry Elam
1784	Michael Angelo Taylor	1947	Henry Josceline Phillimore
1834	William Bond	1954	Malcolm McGougan

ELECTIONS

Democracy was well served in Poole if the number of elections held in the town was any guide. The system of election to the borough council involved one councillor from each ward of the borough retiring each year. As well as these annual elections, which were usually contested, there were by-elections to fill vacancies caused during the year by resignation or death. There were also elections every three years for representatives to serve on Dorset County Council, as well as General Elections.

The Town Clerk and his staff were responsible for preparing the Electoral Roll each year, and for the conduct of elections. Senior members of the council acted as returning officers in borough council elections, and the Sheriff had general oversight of Parliamentary elections. All ward councillors were involved in the election of the ten Aldermen. Five Aldermen were elected every three years. Their term of office on the borough council ran for six years.

The members of the council, despite different political allegiances, generally worked together harmoniously. In 1964, for instance, it was unanimously agreed to bestow the newly constituted honour of Honorary Alderman, for 'exceptional and meritorious service,' on two long-serving Conservative members. Joseph Bright, a champion master baker, had been Mayor during all the war years. William Simmonds, retired director of Butler's department stores, had been Civil Defence Controller during the war and chairman of the Education Committee for many years.

These harmonious relations were changed by the local elections later that year. Labour did well at the polls and gained three seats from the Conservatives. This resulted in 12 Conservative councillors confronting nine Labour and nine Liberal councillors, in a year when five Aldermen came to the end of their six year term.

Four of the five Aldermen retiring that year were senior members of the Council. Arthur Lloyd-Allen was chairman of the Finance Committee, the premier committee of the council, as well as the town's representative on the Association of Municipal Corporations; Geoffrey Bravery was chairman of the Estates Committee and of Poole Conservative Association; Wilfred Haskins, the deputy Mayor, was chairman of the Planning Committee; Mrs Janet Coles was the popular wife of a leading Poole shipping agent and Harbour Commissioner.

All except Alderman Haskins, who preferred to style himself an independent, were Conservative. It was clear that, if the opposition parties joined forces, their 18 votes could transform the hierarchy of the Council by making four of their own members Aldermen. It was well known that they harboured long-standing grievances about the award of committee chairmanships, and elections to the offices of Mayor, Sheriff and Alderman, during the years of Conservative domination.

As soon as it became clear how the Liberal and Labour councillors intended to act, another Conservative Alderman, who had a further three years to serve, volunteered to resign his office if they would agree to re-elect Arthur Lloyd-Allen as Alderman in his place. Harold Byrom, a retired cotton spinner from Lancashire, who had been a member of the Council for 13 years, said: 'But for this contingency, I would not have thought of resigning, but Alderman Lloyd-Allen is a very valuable member of the

Councillor Leslie Cull

council, and it would be disastrous for the town if he were to come off the council at this stage.'

Alderman Byrom's sacrifice was not in vain. The Labour and Liberal councillors helped to re-elect Alderman Lloyd-Allen. The retiring Liberal Alderman, Herbert Ballam, was re-elected for a further six years, but Aldermen Bravery, Haskins and Mrs Coles were voted off. The new Aldermen were Ronald Hart and Leslie Cull, Labour; and Leslie Miller and Richard Garland, Liberal. This left the Aldermanic bench composed of four Conservative, three Labour and three Liberal Aldermen.

For the Conservatives, Alderman Fred Rowe was particularly incensed. 'The six-year term of Aldermen,' he said, 'was to ensure a modicum of continuity. Is it right for members with long, illustrious records to be cast aside to satisfy the ambitions of some who put personal aggrandisement before the interests of this ancient and honourable borough?'

Leslie Miller, one of the new Liberal Aldermen, denied that there had been a pact with Labour members. The Liberals, he said, had always maintained that all parties had a right to fair representation. It was wrong that eight out of ten Aldermen were Conservatives. When they found that their views were shared by the Labour councillors the result was inevitable, and the fault lay with the Conservatives.

The logic of Alderman Miller's argument did nothing to soften the sense of outrage felt by the ex-Aldermen at their summary dismissal from the Council. Geoffrey Bravery, a long serving member, was particularly hurt at being replaced by a councillor who, he claimed, had been on the Council for only two years.

The editor of the *Poole and Dorset Herald* addressed an open letter to Geoffrey Bravery, writing in his newspaper: *When you left Poole Council chamber last week, a victim of parochial party politics, after 21 years' service to the community, hardly anyone stopped to thank you. I know that you and Mrs Bravery, who has been a county councillor for 12 years, have devoted the best part of your lives to serving Poole...it seems tragic that, while still in the prime of life, your activities should end with a brusque dismissal from the Aldermanic bench. After all, the title of Alderman was created to honour loyal service.* He went on to thank Mr Bravery's *fellow victims, who have given unstinting service to Poole.*

The public's reaction to this episode, together with the fading national popularity of the Labour government, might well have been a factor in the council elections of the two years following, when Conservatives gained seats, mainly from the Labour Party. By 1966, Poole Liberal Party was in the grip of a financial crisis, and had lost the

Elizabeth the Second by the Grace of God of the United Kingdom of Great Britain and Northern Ireland and of Our other Realms and Territories Queen Head of the Commonwealth Defender of the Faith To the Returning Officer for the Poole Constituency Greeting **Whereas** by the advice of Our Council We have ordered a Parliament to be holden at Westminster on the **twenty-seventh** day of **October** next WE COMMAND you that due notice being first given you do cause election to be made according to law of a Member to serve in Parliament for the said Poole Constituency And that you do cause the name of such Member when so elected whether he be present or absent to be certified to Us in Our Chancery without delay **Witness** Ourself at Westminster the **twenty-fifth** ..y of **September** in the **thirteenth** year of Our Reign and in the year of Our Lord One thousand nine hundred and **sixty-four.**

COLDSTREAM

To the Returning Officer for the Poole Constituency

A Writ of a new election of a Member for the said Constituency

COLDSTREAM

Crown Office in Chancery, Palace of Westminster

"The Parliamentary Election Writ"

The writ issued to the Borough Returning Officer, commanding him to make arrangements for the election of a Member of Parliament for Poole constituency in the 1964 General Election.

services of its full-time agent. Because of a shortage of funds, it was able to field only three candidates in the council elections that year. Shortly after the 1967 council elections, when Labour did poorly again, Alderman Hart resigned from the Labour Party. As the time approached for the 1970 Aldermanic elections, Alderman Hart also resigned from that office before he could suffer a similar fate to the four Conservatives of 1964.

Conservatives regained overall control of the Council, but the reverberations of 1964 still persisted. In the Aldermanic elections of 1967, Bob Hann, a councillor representing Broadstone, refused to accept nomination for the office of Alderman. He said he had more confidence in the people of Broadstone re-electing him for a further term of office than he had in fellow members of the council!

The last local elections for the old borough council, before the local government reforms of 1974, were held in 1972. The terms of members due to retire after that date were extended until the new council took over. The Labour Party made a small comeback in these elections, winning Newtown ward from the Conservatives, and Upper Parkstone from the Liberals, but the Conservatives kept overall control of the Council.

Mrs Rene Montague, who had been Sheriff in 1970 and was chairman of the Health Committee, was elected Mayor for the last period of the old council's existence. Bert Chaffey, Labour, became what it was believed would be the last person elected Sheriff of Poole. It was not then expected that the office would survive the reformers' zeal.

There were five General Elections held in the town during the decade. The first of these, in October 1964, was notable for the inclusion of two last-minute Parliamentary candidates. Sir Richard Pilkington, the Conservative MP since 1951, was unable to stand again because of continued ill-health, and Oscar Murton, chairman of Poole Conservative Association, and a former borough councillor, was chosen to stand. James Holland, who had fought the previous two elections for the Liberals, astonished his adoption meeting by announcing that he was standing down for business reasons. Herbert Ballam, the deputy Mayor, was adopted in his place.

Results of the General Elections were as follows :

October 1964   *Electorate 66,093*

H O Murton (Conservative)	24,440
H Toch (Labour)	16,158
H C R Ballam (Liberal)	12,224

March 1966   *Electorate 67,787*

H O Murton (Conservative)	25,451
D. A. Sutton (Labour)	19,630
B. Sheriff (Liberal)	8,394

June 1970   *Electorate 78,008*

H O Murton (Conservative)	31,100
I Campbell (Labour)	17,610
M Goode (Liberal)	9,846

February 1974   *Electorate 83,781*

H O Murton (Conservative)	31,156
M Goode (Liberal)	21,088
G Hobbs (Labour)	15,434

October 1974   *Electorate 83,781*

H O Murton (Conservative)	28,982
M Goode (Liberal)	17,557
G Hobbs (Labour)	16,262

GENERALLY

There were many facilities provided for the town, which were initiated by the Council, and then taken over and developed by others, usually the people of Poole themselves. The Sports Centre is an obvious example, but there were others. For instance, the Mayor called the inaugural meeting to consider the formation of a Citizens Advice Bureau. Volunteers, headed by John Culshaw, the chief probation officer, formed Poole CAB, which was formally opened in 1964 by Sir Harold Banwell, the national chairman.

When Frank Gillard, controller of BBC Western Region, wished to establish a remote studio in the Poole area, the Council offered a tenancy of part of the old Branksome Council building. It was here that a BBC production team, supported by local journalists, set up an experimental local radio station. It never went on air, but its output was recorded, primarily as evidence for the Pilkington Committee on the future of sound broadcasting. Responsibility for much of the BBC's sound and television output for the south had already been devolved from Bristol to enlarged studios in Southampton. Local radio was seen as the next stage of devolution. The BBC was eager to retain its sound radio monopoly, and keep local broadcasting out of the hands of commercial operators. The closed-circuit studio at Branksome was run in the same way as a live radio station. The object was to demonstrate that a worthwhile service of news, information and comment could be provided to local communities. To those responsible for supplying the input from the Poole and Bournemouth area, it also demonstrated that local radio could have a voracious appetite for material. That appetite would be limited only by the economics of local broadcasting, and the number of staff a station could afford to employ. Tapes of the closed-circuit broadcasts were used to obtain support for the introduction of local radio, even to the extent of being played to all civic leaders assembled for their annual meeting.

There were many technological changes during the period that affected life in Poole. Postcodes, necessary for the eventual machine-sorting of the post, were quietly introduced into every district in Britain in 1968. In 1972 the 'Hello girls' at telephone exchanges were replaced by automatic dialling. To be prepared for entry into the European Common Market and to facilitate the use of computers in financial transactions, the currency was decimalised in 1971.

The decimalisation of the currency occurred during one of the recurrent periods of inflation and, in the conversion of the old prices to the new decimalised currency, there was a general suspicion among shoppers that the shopkeepers had used the occasion to increase the prices of their goods. The shopkeepers, already feeling threatened by the rise of supermarkets, resented the repeated accusation of profiteering from the change. Mr Stanley Bubb, chairman of Parkstone and District Chamber of Trade, complained that shopkeepers we were 'sick and tired' of continually being branded as robbers. 'In fact, far from making any money out of decimalisation,' be said, ' we are involved in substantial expense, both in training and preparation for the education of the public, which was left almost entirely to us, and also to the purchase of equipment.' Nor could he resist taking a swipe at the supermarkets. 'With present trends,' he added, 'the public will have a choice of pushing trolleys around supermarkets where there is no credit, no advice, no service, and where, far from being able to complain to the owner, in most cases even the staff have no idea who the owner is!'

With the proliferation of colour sets, people began to spend more time watching television. Television improved its local news coverage. One of the results was that anyone wishing to publicise an issue as widely as possible would devise a demonstration which it was hoped would attract television coverage. Television news editors would sometimes take their commitment to the voice of protest beyond the bounds of better judgement. Thus a council tenant who threatened to strew rubbish about the forecourt of the Municipal Buildings, because he had not yet been issued with a free dustbin, might receive the same coverage as campaigners involved in important public issues. These early examples of the 'photo opportunity' began to undermine the traditional news values of printed media.

In 1971, the local Environment Action Group organised a protest about the 'throw away menace' which ended with them dumping a huge pile of non-returnable bottles outside the Schweppes depot in Haymoor Road. The following year, when the Leningrad speedway team came to race against Poole Pirates, a 'silent demonstration' was held outside the Stadium in protest at Russian treatment of Soviet Jewry.

A considerable number of Poole people opposed British entry into the European Economic Community. A 'random referendum' of 750 residents, carried out by a local newspaper, showed 62.8% against entry, with 19.1% undecided. The Anti-Common Market League organised a motorcade, festooned with posters, which proclaimed its message from a loudspeaker van. 'Mr Heath promised no entry into the Common Market without the full-hearted support of both Parliament and the people,' it blared. 'He has not got this support - as he well knows.' The motorcade, formed in Hamworthy, progressed through the centre of Poole and Bournemouth, finishing over two hours later, on Poole Quay.

Poole fishermen were against entry into the Common Market, as it would mean the end of a 12-mile ban on foreign fishermen. In March 1972, dressed in their traditional gear, they sailed their boats to London where they joined a march on Westminster to protest to Parliament.

For many years the borough council had been in a dilemma. To the west, Dorset County Council was pressing for many of Poole's powers to be transferred to it. To the east, Bournemouth Borough Council considered that Poole should be amalgamated with it.

Many Poole people seemed to wish the town to remain independent. For over half a century it had lived in the shadow of its neighbour, dependent on Bournemouth for providing much of its employment, a substantial amount of its shopping, and most of its entertainment. Poole had great expenses in slum clearance, making up roads and re-lighting its streets. However much the Council tried to reduce its rate demand, the burden on a Poole ratepayer was 50% greater than an equivalent householder in Bournemouth.

The Council and its citizens, with a pride in the borough's long history, had long maintained a robust championship of its independence. With 10,000 newcomers moving into Poole every decade, public support of this position was likely to wane over the years.

Perhaps motivated by the recurring overtures of Bournemouth to take over the town, and belated recognition by the Government that local government had to be reformed, or perhaps by the vast increase in the town's holiday visitors with the success of Rockley Sands Holiday Camp, the philosophy of the Council gradually changed. It realised it had important assets that could be exploited to strengthen its standing. Undeveloped land was an advantage that could boost employment in industry and offices. The slum clearance programme would create an opportunity to improve shopping and entertainment facilities. In the medium term, the town could better its financial position, and demonstrate that it was able to stand on its own two feet.

The process of putting such a philosophy into practice in the 1950s and 1960s, resisted by natural suspicion of radical change, vested interests and individual objectors, was inevitably a long one. It was further prolonged by recurring financial crises that confronted the Government of the day.

By 1973, however, the Council could see its plans coming to fruition. Its various achievements are detailed in other sections of this book. They were not, of course, to everyone's approval. One complainant wrote: *Residents know full well that Poole has been turned from an interesting port with very many specially attractive old-world features into a jungle of concrete blocks which certainly have not benefited the people, and lovely country and green areas devastated in spite of protest.*

Bournemouth Chamber of Trade came to appreciate the beneficial effects of these achievements as rates in Poole fell below those in Bournemouth. Its journal commented: *One is forced to wonder if Bournemouth's rate increase is brought about by a mismanagement of public funds...Many will look across the border to Poole and wonder how they have achieved the economic miracle in maintaining the level of rates at a time of escalating costs.*

The local newspaper, its columns for so long full of Poole's turbulent controversies, also approved. *You can feel it in the air in Poole,* it wrote. *It's the excitement of dreams coming true, and new ones being dreamed.* Perhaps the biggest aim of Poole's industrial plan, it continued, was that it was instrumental in the clearly seen need to balance the town's population. Poole saw to it that there were more jobs to bring in young families. In 1960 there were 30,000 Poole residents in employment. In 1971 there were 40,000, a rise of 30% in eleven years. A past complaint had been that Poole did not provide enough white collar jobs and young people had to find work elsewhere. The balance was being redressed, with offices under construction for Barclays, Frizzells, and the Royal National Lifeboat Institution, and other offices at Old Orchard.

It was, though, appropriate that Alderman Lloyd-Allen should sum up these achievements in his last budget speech to the old council before the reorganisation of local government took effect in 1974. He said that at the time of his first speech in 1953, the total rateable value of Poole was £714,000, which was only 34% of that of Bournemouth. Poole's rate was 23s 2d (115.8p) in the pound, 54% greater than that of Bournemouth. At that time, Poole's sewage was pumped into the sea and no slums had been cleared. In 1973, Poole's rate was 3.2p less than that of Bournemouth.

'Credit for this,' he said, 'lies with the Council for its courage in getting so deeply involved in the implementation of the town's development proposals - probably more involved than most towns have ever done; for its tenacity in sticking to its aims, no matter how difficult things became, and bringing so many schemes to a successful conclusion...Better still, often these schemes have provided a capital surplus which has enabled us to provide the town with amenities which, in my early days, we would never have dreamed possible.' They had been provided at no cost to the ratepayers. 'I hope that Canford Heath will provide capital profits to provide for further amenities...'

Poole's pride regained – with an up to date shopping precinct, a bridge over the railway, a restored town centre and a new vitality that promoted business and commercial growth, after years of stagnation.

The ancient ferry that plied between Poole Quay and Hamworthy was revived in the mid–1960s by Jack Stannard, landlord of the Shipwrights' Arms, and boatman Eric Paull.

CULTURE & RECREATION

THE HARBOUR

All kinds of activity in the harbour increased in the 1960s and early 1970s. As well as recreational craft, there were the craft of the Royal Marines, vessels involved in the search for oil at Wytch Farm, and helmsmen training, or taking part in trials, for the Olympic Games. In 1967, some 50 boats and barges of the US Army Floating Equipment Reserve, having been frozen out of their French bases by General de Gaulle, came from St Nazaire to anchor by the side of Wareham Channel.

The increasing number of pleasure craft in the harbour presented the Harbour Commissioners with their greatest problem. They won a battle with the yacht clubs in 1965 to levy a charge on pleasure boats using the harbour but, apart from providing moorings, the Commissioners felt no responsibility to provide other facilities.

In the 1960s most of the Commissioners' revenue was spent on efforts to preserve the Main Channel, which was threatened with silting, and prevent the growth of spartina grass in the harbour. On the other hand, the various currents of the harbour were such that, far from silting, Rat Island was being rapidly eroded. Once 650 feet long and 300 feet wide, it had sheltered the entrance to Parkstone Bay for centuries. By 1969 it had been reduced to 380 by 180 feet and was in danger of being completely overwhelmed. The yachtsman's view of the harbour was dramatically described by Russell Anstey in a speech as Commodore at Parkstone Yacht Club's annual dinner in 1967. He said that *Poole had got the world's worst bloody yachting facilities.*

By that time it was already clear that the yacht marina, proposed by West Sussex Marine Development Company in the early 1960s, was not going to be built. However, in 1970, Poole Harbour Marina Company made a planning application to build a marina off the eastern end of the Quay, extending into Baiter. It was to provide a basin capable of accommodating 860 yachts and incorporating a marine complex, shops, a public house and residential accommodation, and covered an area of 70 acres. The inevitable local objections and the concerns contained in them were voiced in the Council, as well as the County Council. The development would have required an alteration in the approved Town Map. With no decision having been made, the company appealed to the Minister in late 1971 to make a decision.

At the public inquiry, the company's representatives gave evidence that there were then over 6,000 yachts in the harbour, of which 3,100 were lying at moorings; that there was only a single drinking water point available; that refuelling had to be made from a vehicle standing on the Quay; that the only public convenience available was on the Quay, and, moreover, there was not a single electricity point available to yachtsmen.

There was considerable local objection to the marina. Parkstone Yacht Club claimed that the marina would threaten its very existence, and strongly objected to it projecting into the main channel next to the club's sailing area. The Canford Cliffs Land Society claimed that the height of the proposed buildings was excessive, that the proposed flats were incongruous, and, in any case, it opposed any reclamation for residential purposes.

Even so, the Secretary of State, in 1972, approved the building of the marina, subject to the results of the proposed hydrographical survey showing that its construction would have no detrimental effect on the harbour. Meanwhile, the long-running battle of the Council with the owner of Poole Harbour Yacht Club had been effectively won by the owner on his third appeal to the Minister. The club's site protruded into the harbour. The Council was concerned that a large development would have a detrimental effect on the visual amenities of the harbour. It had already refused planning applications for it in 1949 and 1964, which had been confirmed by the Ministry on appeal. It also refused the plan submitted in 1967 that showed a main building 475 feet long by 58 feet wide and a club room of 117 feet by 70 feet. The main building, six times the size of the existing building, included five-storey blocks of 104 flats. The owner argued that, with berths for 236 boats and a car park for 400 cars at the club, the flats were necessary for yachtsmen. His persistence was eventually rewarded in 1968. The Minister overruled the Council's refusal, and granted planning permission for most of the proposals.

THE *TORREY CANYON* DISASTER

In 1967, a threat to the harbour arose which made the continuing arguments about the development of Poole Harbour Yacht Club seem almost irrelevant. The *Torrey Canyon*, a tanker carrying 60,000 tons of crude oil, was wrecked in heavy seas on the Seven Stones Reef off Cornwall on the night of 27 March, 1967. By the following day the ship was breaking up and 30,000 tons of oil had escaped. The great slick of oil was already travelling across St Austell Bay, heading east. It was reported that, with the combination of north winds and spring tides, the slick would reach Poole Bay three days later.

The Government's Standing Emergency Committee met urgently and appointed five Ministers, each to be responsible for various lengths of southern England, stretching from Cornwall to Kent. It announced that the Government would pay three-quarters of the costs incurred by Councils in mitigating the damage or in cleaning up pollution caused by the oil. It was officially considered to be a most serious threat. In fact, the Under Secretary of the Navy said that the slick was 'the greatest peace-time menace to Britain's shores,' and that 'all the extra men and equipment in the world could not deal with the problem.'

Alan Bromby, the National Trust warden on Brownsea Island, immediately called for volunteers to try to save birds polluted by the oil, and Corporation workers were put on day and night stand-by. Captain C H Horn, the Harbour Master, and a co-ordinating committee of boatmen, made plans to meet the slick outside the harbour and spray it with detergent.

Mr Willey, Minister of Land and Natural Resources, was the Minister appointed to be responsible for the Dorset coast. He invited all those responsible for combating the threat to meet him. Representatives of the Harbour Commissioners, yacht clubs, fishermen, police, Royal Marines, and the Town Clerks and Borough Engineers of Poole and Bournemouth, were summoned to an urgent meeting at the Haven Hotel, Sandbanks.

At the meeting the Town Clerk asked whether the Commandant of Royal Marines, Hamworthy considered that a boom could be laid across the harbour mouth to stop the oil entering. The Commandant doubted whether this was possible. The boom laid during the war as a defence against submarines would not have been subject to great tidal pressures in the same way as an oil boom laid on the surface. In view of the seriousness of the situation, though, if the Navy asked the Royal Marines to lay such a boom, they would try hard to do so.

The Town Clerk put the proposition to Mr Wllley, who had a good view from the hotel of the wide vista of the harbour and its islands. The Minister said he appreciated the calamity that might ensue, but he was not sure whether the Admiralty would agree to a boom. He said he would go and talk to them after the meeting. 'We shall have to see what the Admiral says,' he said.

With Bob Hawker, the Borough Engineer, away on holiday, his deputy, Albert Marsden, had been appointed 'Designated Officer' to supervise Poole's response to the threat. He and the Town Clerk decided that as Mr Willey said that 'we would have to see what the Admiral said,' it must mean that they should be present when Mr Willey met him!

In Albert Marsden's car, the two officers fell in behind Mr Willey's car and followed it to Portsmouth. There, they were duly saluted by the guard at the Admiralty headquarters as they followed Mr Willey. Many of the buildings on the site still showed signs of wartime devastation by the Luftwaffe, but the main headquarters building seemed to have survived intact. Mr Willey's car pulled up outside, and he and his staff entered.

It was some time before the Town Clerk and Mr Marsden could find a space to park, but they had no difficulty in entering the building, where the meeting was about to begin. They pushed their way round the door into the crowded room, where the senior officer was sitting at a large desk, looking down at some papers. A number of naval officers were standing round him, and Mr Willey and his small staff were sitting to one side of the table.

The officer in charge of the meeting looked up. 'Who are you?' he demanded suspiciously.

The Town Clerk spoke quickly in an attempt not to be interrupted before he had finished his explanation of the devastating effect a great deal of oil would have in the harbour. He said Mr Willey and he wondered whether in these circumstances, the Admiralty would authorise the Royal Marines to attempt to place a boom across the harbour mouth.

. 'Could it be done, Robert?' the officer asked one of his colleagues. The other man pulled a face and shook his head slowly. 'Pressure of tides too great,' he said.

'The Commandant at Poole said he was willing to try, in view of the gravity ...' the Town Clerk interposed quickly.

'All right, all right, we'll think about it,' the commanding officer said by way of dismissal.

'Well, it was worth a try,' said Albert Marsden resignedly when they got back in the car. It seemed that the Admiralty would refuse to countenance any effort to lay a boom.

Two days later, Albert Marsden rang the Town Clerk. 'You'll never believe it,' he said, 'but a great quantity of 16-inch PVC tubing with a skirt has been delivered.' He said a large contingent of Royal Marines was already busy at Sandbanks, where they were filling the tubing with plastic foam in preparation to sling joined lengths of it across the harbour mouth!

All day the Sandbanks ferry approach was a scene of great activity, watched by press reporters and a small crowd of interested onlookers. The WVS arrived with their canteen. After hours of Herculean effort, the Royal Marines succeeded in preparing more than 500 feet of filled tubing, but when the last of the 75 feet lengths was attached, the holding ropes on the shore broke.

The manufacturers' representatives arrived the following day. They felt the boom would hold if it was anchored with thick nylon ropes. That night, the wind changed direction, blowing the slick out to sea. The crisis had passed, and the project was abandoned.

Many happier and more successful events took place in the harbour than the scare of the *Torrey Canyon*. There were, for instance, regular ceremonies of Beating the Harbour Bounds, which took place in 1961, 1964, 1965, 1968 and 1971. The perambulations of September 1964 and July 1965 were both described in the official programme as celebrating the 600th anniversary of the Winchelsea Certificate, which established Poole's maritime jurisdiction over the harbour and its approaches. The year of the Certificate was given in both programmes as 1365, a date which also appears on a frieze in the Council Chamber commemorating important events in Poole's history. Bernard Short, the former borough archivist, was adamant that the correct date was 1364. His view was supported by the Council's annual report, published in May 1965. An item headed *600th anniversary of Beating of the Bounds* recorded the 1964 perambulation. It was followed by a historical note which gave the date as 1364, and ended enigmatically: *There will be an extra ceremony this year to mark the 600th anniversary of the granting of the Winchelsea Certificate*. Though it might have been hard to see how a 600th anniversary could be celebrated two years running, nobody seemed to mind. In a time of rapid transformation, the citizens of Poole were eager to proclaim their ancient rights, traditions and ceremonies, and to encourage newcomers to preserve them. The annual report of the Corporation for 1968 gave the date of the Winchelsea

Members of the jury line the way as the Mayor (Bob Hann) leads the procession to the balcony of the Custom House for the start of the 1968 ceremony of beating the bounds of Poole Harbour. He is followed by the deputy Town Clerk (Bob Cass), the Rector of Poole (Canon Tom Livermore) and the Borough Librarian (Leonard Shaw).

Certificate as April 26, 1364, and that year was quoted in the official programme for the 1971 perambulation.

Shortly before the perambulation in September 1964 a discovery was made in the harbour which threw an even longer perspective on its antiquities. A Harbour Board dredger working in Brownsea Roads brought up a wooden object more than 23 feet long, which proved to be the stern section of an ancient dug-out canoe. A further section of the hull, of similar length, was recovered from the seabed, with the help of skin divers, a few days later. The two sections had severed diagonally along the length of the hull. When put together they showed that the canoe had been carved from a single log of oak. It had an overall length of 33 feet and was four feet wide at the stern. The canoe was later carbon-dated to approximately 295 BC. It was kept under water in a polythene lined trench in the garden of Scaplen's Court until a permanent 2,000 gallon tank was provided inside the building early in 1965. Here, it proved a considerable attraction to visitors. Their numbers increased to 20,672 in 1965, and 18,990 in 1966, from 11,484 in 1964.

The dug-out canoe in Poole Harbour Commissioners' yard before it was taken to Scaplen's Court for preservation.

Top: Robin Aisher, Iain Macdonald Smith, Rodney
Pattisson and Paul Anderson.
Right: The Mayor (Bob Hann) presents a specially
commissioned Poole Pottery plaque to Rodney Pattisson.

In 1965 the Royal Motor Yacht Club was the base for a two-week regatta for leading Olympic helmsmen, followed by the final selection trials in 1972. The RMYC also hosted International offshore powerboat races in 1968. Truckline Ferries inaugurated their roll-on roll-off freight-only service between Poole and Cherbourg in 1973. Two young Poole men were chosen for the crew of Edward Heath's yacht *Morning Cloud*. Two Poole yachtsmen competed in the *Observer* Single-handed Transatlantic Race. They were Brian Cooke, a Parkstone bank manager, and Mike McMullen of the Royal Marines. Three of the yachts taking part in the race were built in Poole by Southern Ocean Shipyard.

Poole yachtsmen distinguished themselves in the nineteenth Olympic Games held in Mexico in 1968. Lieutenant Rodney Pattisson RN and Iain Macdonald Smith won the gold medal in the Flying Dutchman Class in *Superdocious*. Robin Aisher won the bronze medal in the 5.5 metre class in *Yeoman XV* with his crew, Paul Anderson and Adrian Jardine. John Glavin of Poole reached the semi-final of the 1,000-metre single-handed canoeing event. Sergeant Notley, then of the Green Howards, reached the final of the Biathlon event in the Winter Olympics. Brian Cooke, a member of Lilliput

Sailing Club, Poole, sailed his sloop *Opus 1* into third place on handicap in the *Observer* Single-handed Transatlantic race from Plymouth to Rhode Island in 1968.

To celebrate these outstanding yachting successes the Council held a civic banquet at which specially commissioned Poole Pottery plaques were presented by Bob Hann, the Mayor, to Rodney Pattisson and Robin Aisher and their crews, and to Brian Cooke. Sadly, Brian Cooke was later lost at sea, in circumstances never fully explained, while on another single-handed voyage in the Atlantic.

The Olympic Sailing Association was eager to set up its sailing headquarters in Poole Harbour but it abandoned plans to build one near Bay View, Sandbanks, when local residents complained. When similar objections were made to an alternative site near Evening Hill it abandoned its plans and set it up in Weymouth.

The public had many different, often conflicting, interests in the harbour. Some sections were interested in sailing or boating; others in fishing or water sports, and others in nature conservation, or simply enjoying the views. Those whose homes had harbour views were particularly eager to retain them. For this reason, there was virtually no development proposal in or near the harbour that did not create some objection.

Poole's first mobile public library.

THE LIBRARY SERVICE

In 1960 the Poole Library service operated from the Central Library in South Road (now Lagland Street) and from six branch libraries. Five of these lending libraries were in converted buildings, such as at Oakdale, where two discarded mobile classrooms were used, or at Newtown, in the old church hall at the Church of the Good Shepherd. Outlying areas of the borough, such as Merley and Bearwood, and the new council estates at Waterloo and Turlin Moor, were still not served by a conveniently situated library. In 1964, the Corporation bought a mobile library to establish a weekly service to these districts.

For eight decades since Poole's public library service began in 1885 the Corporation had never provided a purpose-built library for its residents. Its two permanent purpose-built library buildings had both been given by private benefactors. The central library in South Road was erected by J J Norton in 1887, and Branksome Branch library was given by Andrew Carnegie, the Scottish philanthropist, to Branksome Urban District Council in 1903, the year before Branksome became part of the borough of Poole.

In 1965, the Council erected its first purpose-built library, Rossmore branch library, in Herbert Avenue. Later that year it built Hamworthy branch library in Blandford Road, adjoining Herbert Carter School, and bought land adjoining Broadstone car park for a permanent library to replace the one temporarily housed at 'Milbourne.'

Plans to replace the obsolescent Central Library had been frustrated by wars and lack of funds since 1934. In 1966, the Libraries Committee was suddenly presented

Hamworthy branch library.

The new Rossmore library in Herbert Avenue, Parkstone.

with the prospect of achieving its ambitions in the proposed Arndale shopping centre. Not only that, but the Redevelopment Committee even offered to pay for the new building from its accumulated capital profits.

The committee had no regrets in abandoning its earlier plans to build the new library in the Civic Centre. The new site, in what was intended to become the commercial centre of the town, was very attractive to the Committee. It immediately accepted the Redevelopment Committee's suggestion.

Plans for the new building, prepared by the Borough Architect and Borough Librarian, provided for a floor area of 28,700 square feet. This was more than four times the area of Norton's library in South Road, built when the population of Poole was a mere 12,310. The new library allowed the provision of additional books, as well as extra services, such as a music library, a study, an area for children, a local collections department, a meeting room, and an exhibition gallery.

The building work began as soon as the foundations and the first floor of the Arndale Centre had been erected. The new Central Library was opened on May 1, 1970. It soon attracted many new users of the library service. In its first year's operation it made 320,000 more issues than the old library in South Road, with only a slight drop in the number of issues by branch libraries.

In February 1971, less than a year after this achievement, the council had the first intimation that it was to lose its libraries. In that month the Government published a White Paper on proposals for the future of local government. It proposed that Bournemouth, Christchurch, and some areas of Hampshire should be joined to Dorset and administered by a new Dorset County Council which would, among other things, take over Poole's public libraries.

Top: The spacious, airy interior of the new Central Library was a world away from the Victorian premises in South Road.
Below: Another view of the main floor of the library.

When the Local Government Act came into effect on April 1, 1974, the Corporation would have no library powers. This did not affect the responsibility for the town's museum service. The borough council had been responsible for this since 1890, when J J Norton presented the town with the small museum adjoining the central library, in celebration of the visit of the Prince of Wales to open Poole Park.

Responsibility for this service was transferred to the Parks Committee, which entered into a contract to renovate the Guildhall to replace the old museum in South Road. John Dockerill was appointed the town's first full-time Museum Curator. The forthcoming transfer of powers to the county council also raised another problem. It had always been considered that the Borough Librarian was the appropriate officer to be responsible for the borough's archive collection, and he had been appointed Deputy Borough Archivist. The Council thought that, with the library service transferred to the county council, it would not be appropriate for the officer of another authority to have this responsibility. The Council therefore transferred custody of the archive collection to the Town Clerk, as Honorary Borough Archivist.

SPORTS CENTRE

When Poole Borough Council was informed by the developers that they could not meet the original terms of their agreement to build the Arndale shopping centre, an early meeting with Mr Sam Chippendale, managing director of the company, was arranged. The news that a ten-pin bowl could not be included in the precinct did not come as a surprise. Arthur Lloyd-Allen, Chairman of the Committee, had learned earlier that franchises were granted on the basis of population. As a licence had been granted for a bowling centre in Poole Road, Branksome, no further franchise would be granted in Poole. Although some of the facts quoted by Mr Chippendale could be queried, there was no gainsaying that building costs had increased by at least 10% in the long period which had elapsed since the original draft lease was agreed. Nor could it be denied that the rents for shopping premises were depressed.

Those negotiating with the company approached the meeting in a pragmatic way. Mr Chippendale was desperate not to damage his company's reputation. The Corporation's negotiators were adamant that his suggested solution to omit the uneconomic features - by which be meant all the upper floors of the development - was not acceptable. The shopping precinct would become the centre of the town. It was essential for it to have height, as well as to provide some social amenities.

While Arndale was in trouble over a franchise for the bowling centre, the Town Clerk met Douglas Insole, a leading cricketer and a member of the National Sports Council, who told him it was promoting the provision of purpose-built sports centres. Harlow Development Company had set up a trust, which was building such a centre, and the Ministry of Education had made a substantial grant towards the cost.

As part of the tentative agreement, Mr Chippendale offered to pay any trust that was formed in Poole half the cost of building a 'one-court' centre, then estimated at £120,000. His company would be responsible for providing foundations sufficient for such a building and would grant a sub-lease of the site for the period of its own lease of the land.

It was left to Arthur Lloyd-Allen to put the proposition to the Council. With the Arndale company contributing £60,000, and a possible £30,000 grant from the Ministry, the Council would have a sports centre for a cost of only £30,000. If a Poole Sports Council could be set up to make an application, it could also raise funds towards the cost of the building. 'It is my own view,' be concluded, 'that, if you accept...you will have a finer commercial centre in prospect than you have ever had.' Some members were fearful of future losses by a sports centre, but it was agreed to consider the matter and arrange to apply for a grant from the Ministry.

Wilfred Haskins, lately Chairman of the Planning Committee, and Fred Rowe, the Chairman of the Amenities and Recreation Committee, were both enthusiastic supporters of the Sports Centre. The Mayor, Alderman Ronald Hart, called a meeting of all sports organisations in the town, which formed the Poole Sports Council. A Sports Centre Committee was elected by the newly-formed council. The committee decided, at its first meeting, to apply to become a sporting charity to raise the balance of the necessary money. Arthur Lloyd-Allen was elected president; Wilfred Haskins, chairman; Fred Rowe, vice-chairman; George Kendall, manager of the Midland Bank in High Street, treasurer, with the Town Clerk as secretary. The trust also invited a number of Poole's sporting celebrities to be vice-presidents. Wilfred Rhodes, the cricketer; Peter Alliss, the golfer; Jeanne Bisgood, twice English ladies golf champion; Betty Uber, Britain's most famous Badminton player; and Courtney Jones, twice world ice dance champion, all accepted the invitation.

By January, 1967, the Trust had been formally established and the appeals committee was ready to begin its campaign. By this time the committee had decided that Poole would need a larger, 'two court' centre, which meant that an estimated sum of £192,500 would be required. After the developer's contribution of £60,000, the grant from the Ministry of £35,000, and a grant of £50,000 from the Corporation's capital profits, a sum of £47,500 had to be raised from the public before the contract to build the centre could be signed. What was more, it would have to be raised quickly, before the foundations for the central part of the building were laid.

Despite the Government freeze on wages and its severe restrictions on all building work over £50,000, it had promised to grant the Arndale company a licence on February 1, 1967. The appeal committee agreed to open its appeal on January 13, 1967, with a 'Sportsman's Ball' at Rockley Sands Holiday Camp.

A local printer donated 35,000 pamphlets making *an urgent appeal to all who are proud of Poole* and the enthusiasm with which the sporting community threw itself into the appeal was most heartening. Even sportsmen and women who were hardly likely to use the centre, such as Colin Chataway and A F Kirkcaldy, the captain and vice-captain of Broadstone Golf Club, Ron Francis, the organiser of Poole Boxing Club. and the secretary of Poole Archery Club, became enthusiastic and active fund raisers.

Despite all these efforts, the appeal would need many large donations from individuals or companies if the sum was to be raised in time.

When Alderman Fred Rowe, the chairman of the appeals committee, was elected

Work in progress on the section of the Arndale Centre that would accommodate a new Central Library and Sports Centre.

Mayor in May that year, he adopted the sports centre as his official charity. He threw himself energetically into the appeal. He used to say that if friends saw him coming down the road they would cross over to avoid being fleeced for more money. However, many of the more affluent citizens of Poole were not unhappy to enter into covenants to pay £250 a year for four years. This entitled the Trust, as a registered charity, to claim the return of tax on the amounts paid.

Mainly through the energy of Fred Rowe, considerable sums were raised .Many smaller amounts came from events specially arranged by the town's sporting associations and collections at sporting events.

The great bulk of the money was raised locally. Applications were made to many national funds, but most of them were already fully committed. The one exception was the Wolfson Foundation. Nothing was heard for some months until one day, Sir Charles Wolfson called unexpectedly at the Municipal Buildings. When it became apparent that Sir Charles had called in answer to the Town Clerk's letter, seeking a grant, he was taken into the Mayor's Parlour.

As the Mayor, who was chairman of the appeal committee, began a well rehearsed introduction to his request for a donation, Sir Charles interrupted. He said he had been told all about the appeal by the taxi driver who brought him from the station. If a taxi driver knew all about it and was enthusiastic for its success, Sir Charles said, that was enough to convince him. His foundation would make a contribution of £4,750 which was 10% of the appeal total. It was the largest single contribution made to the appeal.

By November that year, building the main block of the shopping centre was about to begin. The strength of the foundations would depend on whether the sports centre project was to go ahead. The architects needed a definite decision soon. The Committee had raised well over £20,000 and believed it could raise the balance by the time the building had been completed. It agreed that the contract for the centre should be executed.

With the die cast, the Committee redoubled its efforts: but its very enthusiasm led to one impasse. English's garage donated a new car, which the Committee felt would make an attractive prize in a draw. The sports clubs, members of the committee and their spouses, sold tickets enthusiastically, even attending dances at Rockley Sands Holiday Camp to sell them to departing holiday makers.

Then, one morning, Arthur Hambleton, the Chief Constable of Dorset, telephoned the Town Clerk. 'Could I come and see you this morning?' he asked. 'Sorry, Chief, can't cope this morning,' the Town Clerk said, 'I've just got back from holiday, and I'm ...'

'Sorry, I've got to insist,' interrupted the Chief Constable, 'it's important.'

When the Chief Constable arrived, his manner seemed unusually formal. He produced a draw ticket. 'This is your name at the bottom of the ticket as the promoter, isn't it?' he asked the Town Clerk. 'Well, I've come here personally to reprimand you for running an illegal lottery, and tell you that it will have to be cancelled.'

One of the Corporation's most persistent critics had made a point about the law as it then stood. Curious as it may seem in these days, when lottery prizes run into millions of pounds, it was illegal in 1967, under the Lotteries Act, 1963, to offer a prize of more than £100. An exception was made for 'competitions' which could be said to involve the exercise of some skill or judgement - such as estimating the total attendance at a national motor show! The guardians of public morality, some of them self-appointed, still insisted upon the merit of such fine, pedantic, distinctions, and the law, as it stood, had to be upheld.

It was, therefore, 'a fair cop' by the Chief Constable. Tickets were withdrawn from sale, purchasers were offered their money back, and the prize was reduced to £100. A few were angry and disappointed as, indeed, were the organisers, who did not make as much money as they had hoped.

Members of the Sports Trust, far from being dismayed, decided to celebrate the 90th birthday of their vice-president, Wilfred Rhodes, and the signing of the contract to build the sports centre, at a gala dinner at the Branksome Tower Hotel on November 16, 1967.

Tickets for the dinner sold out quickly. A A Thompson, Wilfred Rhodes' favourite sports writer on the *Yorkshire Post*, came down from Yorkshire to propose the main toast to Mr Rhodes; Colin Cowdrey, then captain of the English XI, telephoned with best wishes, and the other vice-presidents, officers and members of the Trust and the borough council all combined to make it a memorable evening.

Inflation was continuing to push up building costs. Arndale, the Corporation and the Ministry all agreed to increase their grants, while the amount required from the public appeal increased to £62,000. On completion of the building, the Committee was still some £10,000 short of its new target. Happily the developers agreed not to press

The versatile nature of the multi-purpose sports hall, with bowls, badminton and physical training in progress.

for the balance, and arrangements were made for the official opening of the Sports Centre.

Denis Howell, the Minister of Sport, performed the opening ceremony on September 11, 1969. He was fulsome in congratulating the Trust, the developers and the Corporation for their contributions. Poole had taken the lead, be said, in providing a model of partnership between local government, sports clubs, the public and government which be hoped other towns would follow.

The previous June the Trust had suffered the death of its chairman, Wilfred Haskins. Alderman Rowe replied to the Minister's opening speech, pointing out there was still a balance of more than £8,000 to be found before the centre could finally be free of debt.

The opening ceremony was followed by demonstrations by international and county representatives in fencing, judo, archery, football, tennis and weight training. Similar programmes were held for squash, badminton, basketball, table tennis, rifle shooting and cricket on subsequent evenings that week. The centre was opened for general use the following week.

The completion of the building did not lessen the efforts to raise the balance of the sum required by the Trust. It had almost been raised by September, 1971, when Towngate Bridge had been completed, and was due to be officially opened on

At the opening of the Sports Centre a young David Owen, MP, discusses with the Town Clerk the prospects for a similar venture in his Plymouth constituency.

Those who walked over Towngate Bridge before it was opened to traffic in 1971 received a certificate signed by the Mayor in return for a donation to the Sports Centre appeal.

Sport for all – the theme of the mural outside the entrance to Poole Sports Centre.

Play in progress during the En-Tout-Cas tennis tournament at the Sports Centre.

Councillor John Norman

September 30. Pedestrians would be banned from using it. It was thought that many would appreciate a chance to walk over the bridge and enjoy the views from it before it was opened to traffic. For a few hours on the Sunday before the opening, members the public were allowed to walk over the bridge on payment of a small contribution to the appeal. Hundreds of people did so, and each received a souvenir certificate, signed by the Mayor and the chairman of the Trust.

Shortly after the centre opened, the National Association of Town Clerks of England held their annual conference in Poole. Because of the calling of a General Election, Peter Walker, the Local Government Minister, had to cancel his attendance and speech to the conference. The Town Clerk was asked to use the vacant space in the agenda to show the delegates round the Arndale Centre and the sports centre.

As part of this tour the sports centre manager was asked to outline to the delegates how the Trust had arranged the various programmes for the use of the centre. The Town Clerk was already a little perturbed at the visit, fearing questions about the financial returns, which were most disappointing.

The Trustees had been having problems. Attendances were most gratifying, but the centre was not paying its way. The gaming machines, the 'one-armed bandits,' supposed to guarantee a profit, were losing money, as were the licensed bar and coffee shop.

The trustees, in seeking a manager, had concentrated on ability to teach sports, and most of the advertisements had been in education journals. The manager appointed was a good sportsman and teacher. It was not his fault that he had less experience or aptitude for management.

The trustees had begun to think that the centre needed a manager with business experience. The Town Clerk was astounded when Fred Rowe, their chairman, revealed that he had sacked the manager the day before the visit by conference delegates. 'You can't do that!' the Town Clerk exclaimed. 'Can't help that,' replied the Chairman, 'I've bloody well done it!'

The Town Clerk was relieved that the manager seemed to feel no resentment and was still happy to give his talk to the Town Clerks. It had a remarkable outcome. The Town Clerk was approached by the Town Clerk of a large northern town. He said he normally disliked poaching staff, but now that the sports centre was up and running, it could probably continue without its present manager. As his council was thinking of building a number of such centres, he had offered the manager at Poole a job, which he had accepted!

These early troubles were resolved after the appointment of John Norman as Secretary to the sports trust. He had recently come to live in Poole after retiring as a bank manager in Aden. John Loose (later to become the manager of the centre) was appointed manager of the bar and coffee shop.

The Trust then went from success to success. For some time it was, with Harlow, one of only two purpose-built sports centres in the country, and it attracted a number of national sporting events. In December 1969, the National Badminton Championships were held there. In 1970 the En Tout Cas tennis circuit finals were covered by the BBC commentators Dan Maskell and John Barrett. A newcomer, Evonne Goolagong, Australian champion, was beaten by the British Number 1, Mrs Joyce Willing, and the Czech, Jaan Kukai, won the men's event. The sports centre also staged the national finals of the Daily Express five-a-side boys' football competition.

At the end of the first year the sports centre made a loss of some £900. In the second year it made a profit of over £1,400 and, in its first 25 years, unlike many centres subsequently built, it never needed a rate subsidy. In fact it has extended the original centre, built another centre at Broadstone and taken over the running of a centre in Christchurch. It fulfilled all the early hopes of the original trustees and all the many helpers who rallied to the cause.

BAITER

In 1966, the Corporation completed the first stage of its reclamation at Baiter. With the use of some 400,000 cubic yards of overburden from local clay pits, 30 acres of land had been produced. This was graded and seeded, and opened for use by the public, for whom a car park for 230 cars was provided.

It was not until 1968 that the Council was able to resume reclamation work. At that time large quantities of pulverised refuse were being produced by the new refuse disposal works. It drained well, and was ideal for use in reclamation. It also saved the considerable costs of the purchase and transport of other filling material, which would have required a loan sanction from the Ministry. Even so, it took three years and 210,000 cubic yards of pulverised refuse to complete the reclamation.

It was then possible to link Poole Park and Baiter by a pedestrian subway under the railway line at the end of Park Lake Road. Putting the prefabricated concrete sections in place under the Whitecliff railway embankment required temporary closure of the line. The only time at which this could be done, British Rail stated, was after the 11.30pm train from Waterloo to Weymouth passed on Christmas Eve, and before the 5.30pm train from Weymouth was due on Boxing Day.

In the early hours of Christmas Day, 1971, teams from British Rail lifted the track and disconnected the multicore signal and telephone cables. Immediately this had been done, workmen started excavating the railway embankment down to the level required for the subway.

The stages of reclamation between Baiter and Whitecliff.

Tunnelling under the railway embankment to provide a pedestrian subway between Poole Park and Baiter.

Further reclamation between Baiter and Whitecliff opened pleasant views across the harbour to motorists, but also created fears of a new main road between the Old Town and Whitecliff.

It took the whole of Christmas Day for a second shift of workmen to complete this work and lower the five 22-ton concrete units into place. Ducts were laid to carry drainage and electrical services through the embankment. After that, it took a third shift of workers to backfill the tunnel, reform the embankment and spread stone ballast ready for the railway track to be relaid.

At 2.30pm on Boxing Day, British Rail gangs returned to relay the track and reconnect signalling cables. The 5.30pm train to Waterloo passed safely, and the men were able to go home and rejoin the Christmas festivities.

That year the Royal Institute of Chartered Surveyors awarded the Corporation a Certificate of Commendation for the reclamation of Baiter, as 'being of merit and worthy of public recognition.'

Not all the plans for Baiter went as well. Proposals for a road connection to link the Old Town to Whitecliff were opposed by some residents in Whitecliff. The Minister, in approving the development of Baiter, excluded from his approval the design of a road between Baiter and Sandbanks Road. There was another setback following a public inquiry. The Inspector decided that the amount of land to be designated as open space, to replace the three-quarters of an acre taken from Whitecliff Recreation Ground for the new road, was insufficient. When the old Borough Council was dissolved in 1974 it had still not obtained planning approval for the road, although the line of part of it had been temporarily surfaced.

ROCKLEY HOLIDAY CAMP AND TOURISM

The development of Rockley Sands Holiday Camp was nearing completion when Tom Sherrin, the Mayor, opened the bar in the Palladium in 1964. It was already attracting 100,000 holiday visitors each year - more than all Poole's hotels, guest houses, holiday flats and furnished accommodation put together - and having an impact on trade in local shops.

The Corporation's first objective in providing the Rockley camp was not so much to give a fillip to the tourist trade as to control the spate of planning applications to establish camping sites on many vacant spaces in the borough. There were other camps in the county for which the local authority had insufficient powers of control to ensure that they would not detract from the amenities. Poole's Planning Committee argued that if the Corporation owned the land it could, under landlord's covenants, control how the camp was set out and maintained.

Much to the chagrin of Peter Arney, the long-suffering Publicity Officer, the Corporation made no real efforts to encourage tourism. One consequence had been that even before the second world war, the borough's principal hotels chose to promote themselves as being in Bournemouth, some even paying to have a Bournemouth telephone number.

By 1964, most of these Poole hotels had become sites for new blocks of flats, and with Rockley Sands successfully promoting itself, the Council felt no great need to try to attract more holidaymakers. Poole's roads and beaches seemed full enough of visitors.

A summer's day at Branksome Chine. Poole jealously guarded its miles of golden sands from attribution to the adjoining borough of Bournemouth, but did little during the period to advance its own status as a holiday resort.

There was also an underlying fear that the more Poole promoted itself as a tourist resort, the more it would align itself with Bournemouth and encourage its repeated attempts to absorb Poole.

Poole's pride in its attractions would never allow it to stand on one side and ignore the tourist completely. Its Publicity and Information Service produced and distributed some 17,000 official guides each year, and helped visitors to find accommodation in the town.

Visit Bournemouth but stay in Poole was one of the hopeful holiday slogans of the time. Those who did so were far outnumbered by visitors to Poole who stayed elsewhere, as the figures compiled each year by the Publicity Officer showed. In 1971 the totals of visitors to principal tourist attractions were as follows:

Compton Acres	136,000	Miniature railway	180,351
Scaplen's Court	13,964	Boating lake	110,001
Brownsea Island	92,000	Children's zoo	85,276
Merley Tropical Bird Gardens	36,000	Juvenile amusements,	
Putting and crazy golf	138,000	Sandbanks	190,188

Vision of the future: a preliminary sketch for the facade of Poole Arts Centre.

ARTS CENTRE

With growing public interest in the arts, the Government produced a White Paper in 1965 on 'Housing the Arts', which stated that 'the enjoyment of the arts should not be regarded as something remote from everyday life' and encouraged the provision of 'places where the best of the arts may be made available...and where facilities may be provided for all artistic and further educational activities.' As early as 1966 the Libraries Committee suggested that its vacant library buildings in South Road might be converted to such a purpose, but they were considered to be too small to make an effective centre. It also suggested that the Guildhall could become a picture gallery.

The town had required a large hall for meetings or entertainment ever since the early 1930s, when the Council lost its nerve over plans for a town hall on the Civic Centre site, even though the Government promised a generous contribution to its cost. More central, purpose-built premises were now required. A site for a proposed police station on the corner of Kingland Road and Seldown Lane, was suggested, but councillors were warned that an arts centre might cost £400,000 to build and at least a 2p rate to run.

Alan Hutchinson, Principal of Poole Technical College, enthusiastically supported the scheme, and with his colleagues did his best to meet the cultural aspirations of Poole people. He formed Poole College Music Society, which presented concerts by nationally known musicians. The series opened in October 1968 with a piano recital by Denis Matthews. More than 100 people opted to become vice-presidents of the Society by booking up for the rest of its programme. The local press commented: *Very few of the 400 or so present could have recalled accurately the last time Poole was offered a musical event of this stature. A fair guess was between 10 and 20 years ago.* In July 1970 the college promoted a week's Festival of Arts, at which visitors were invited to sign a petition calling for a permanent venue for the arts. Antony Hopkins unveiled a statue, *Aloe*, by Barbara Hepworth, in the college grounds. The Council, shortly afterwards, appointed a special sub-committee to report on all aspects of providing an arts centre.

The chief officers prepared a detailed report following consultations with local arts groups and associations on what they would like to see provided for the town. Inquiries were also made of many local authorities who had already provided arts centres, as well as the Arts Council of Great Britain, Southern and South Western Arts, the Society of Theatre Consultants, the British Film Institute, the British Theatre Technicians, the BBC and Southern Television.

The report summarised the requests that had been made for the centre and indicated what the officers felt could reasonably be included. The need for a large hall with seating for concerts and general entertainment and a hall with a flat floor for dinners, dances and pop concerts was overcome by an ingenious plan devised by the Borough Engineer and his staff. It provided for the raked concert floor, with its seats, to slide below the stage and its dressing rooms, to leave the auditorium with a flat floor.

The capital cost of the building at 1972 prices was estimated at £1.004 million and the running costs, based on the experience of other municipal arts centres, at £85,000 a year. If the estimated cost of the building was borrowed it would cost an additional £60,000 a year. On the other hand, the Corporation could use its profits from its capital investments, which could amount to £792,000, by the time the centre was built. That would leave only some £200,000 to fund, which would cost £12,000 a year in loan charges. Another £7,000 a year would be debited to the running costs to make up for the amount of interest previously credited against the committee's expenses. That would increase the effective running costs of such a centre to £104,000 a year, equal to an increased rate of 1.6 pence in the £. The report sounded a warning that some land which was expected to enhance the council's capital receipts would probably have to be transferred if the council lost its highway powers in a reorganisation of local government. Furthermore, capital receipts already achieved from the exercise of powers which were transferred to another authority, would probably also have to be surrendered.

Preliminary sketch plans for an Arts Centre to be built in Kingland Road were produced in 1968. They provided for an auditorium, exhibition room, meeting room and rehearsal or general purpose rooms. The Council approved them in principle, subject to local interest and support being tested at a public meeting.

There were many problems about providing for all the uses requested by local arts organisations. Kenneth Matchett, general manager of the Western Orchestral Society, wanted rehearsal facilities for the Bournemouth Symphony Orchestra and Sinfonietta, and for occasional performances in the main hall. Relations between Bournemouth

Borough Council and the orchestras had again become strained, not least over the dual use of the Winter Gardens for symphony concerts, summer shows and rehearsals during the holiday season. Rehearsals in the Arts Centre's main hall would solve the problem of finding a use for it during the mornings. It was felt, though, that if concerts were also to be given there, the hall's capacity should be increased. It was agreed that the Western Orchestral Society should contribute to the cost of the centre, but this required the approval of the Arts Council. It took some time to agree these arrangements. Meanwhile, the Society expanded its requests to include the provision of an administrative headquarters on the site.

The difficulty was that the orchestras depended upon the Arts Council of Great Britain for their funding. Its chairman was most sympathetic and encouraging when he met Mr Matchett and the Town Clerk, but explained that the Arts Council, in turn, was entirely dependent upon a Government grant, which varied from year to year. Thus, he explained, it was never able to promise anything in advance. Eventually, the Western Orchestral Society felt able to promise a contribution of £175,000, and the Arts Council provisionally set aside £50,000.

It was not until February 1972, that Alderman Lloyd-Allen could bring the final proposals to the Council, which approved them. 'I can think of no finer ending to the present work of the Borough Council before it goes out of existence in 1974 than the provision of the Arts Centre,' he said. He added that the rate burden would be little more than a penny rate, and the sub-committee would not wish to go ahead with it unless there was sufficient public support. Not all the members agreed. Alderman Steptoe felt it was on the wrong site. Councillor Mrs Edna Adams felt that one meeting of the council was insufficient to agree such a development. One or two others felt that the money should be spent on other things.

The promised public meeting took place in April 1972, in the main hall of the Technical College. It was then the largest hall in the borough. It seated 500, but was not large enough to hold all those who attended. Over 200 others were accommodated in two halls on the floor beneath, which were connected by closed circuit television.

A brochure was prepared by the Town Clerk to accompany the public meeting with a preliminary sketch of a proposed Arts Centre, and drawings to show alternative accommodation. Plan A would cost £1.002 million and Plan B £1.43 million. The Town Clerk outlined what a multi-purpose centre might provide. It would be *a centre where you can watch a play or a film, listen to music, have a meal or a drink, paint a picture, practise your music, throw a pot, develop your holiday snaps or your interest in, say, local history; attend a dance or look at modern sculpture - all in one building.* He reported that grants from the Arts Council and the British Film Institute amounting to £60,500 had been promised. If Plan A was adopted and the estimated £800,000 of capital receipts and rate fund balances were used, it would cost £104,000 a year, the equivalent to a rate of 1.6p in the pound. Plan B, if the Bournemouth Orchestras were able to find the money for their administrative headquarters and additional accommodation in the concert hall, would cost slightly less.

Alderman Lloyd-Allen proposed the motion to agree to the building of the centre. He said that to prepare working drawings and go out to tender for the building would

Councillor Mrs Edna Adams

take until the last half of 1973, with a contract period of December 1973 to March 1976. He pointed out that the council had already provided a sports centre, and a swimming bath would soon be completed. Should not these facilities be complemented by the Arts Centre? he asked. It would add another dimension to the quality of life in Poole. 'True,' he ended, 'no one has ever died through lack of art, but, throughout history, civilised man has regarded art as adding a dimension to the quality of life.'

Geoffrey Hopkinson, the Borough Architect, explained the plans as they were projected on to a screen, and members of the public were invited to express their views.

The *Poole and Dorset Herald* reported: 'Nearly 800 raised arms proclaimed an overwhelming 'Yes' to the Council's Poole Centre for the Arts concept...Only five showed opposition to the scheme.'

One or two members of the council were inclined to disregard the result of public consultation. When the scheme came before the Council later in April 1972, Councillor Derrick Green claimed that the meeting had been unrepresentative and that opponents had not been given enough time to mobilise support. Councillor Mrs Adams, never short of an headline-catching remark, suggested that a vote for the arts centre 'would change the emblem of Poole from a dolphin to a white elephant.' She branded the project as reckless and ill-considered, and declared that community centres for Bear Cross, Creekmoor, Turlin Moor and Merley were more important. Other members thought the wrong site had been chosen. Alderman Steptoe suggested it should be built at Upton House. For all that, no one voted against the adoption of the scheme, although there were four abstentions. The approval was subject to the final proposals being accepted at a further public meeting.

The Festival of Music and Arts at the Technical College that July was an even more impressive event than usual. Under the banner of *Carrying the torch for Poole*, it began in celebratory mood, with a fanfare of trumpets by the Royal Corps of Signals. Richard Baker from the BBC opened the festival, which included excerpts from Shakespeare's plays; exhibitions of ballet; oboe, piano and harpsichord recitals, and a concert by the Bournemouth Sinfonietta.

The second public meeting, in October 1972, was a much smaller affair, with some 200 people in the audience at Poole Technical College. By then, the Police Authority had agreed to sell the site in Kingland Road to the Council, and the estimate of the final cost had begun to rise. Alderman Lloyd-Allen reported that with inflation, and extra work required to accommodate the Bournemouth orchestras, as much as £430,000 would have to be added to the estimate, bringing it to £2.5 million.

Councillor Mrs Adams' husband, Ivor, a retired bank manager, joined in the attack, claiming that a simpler scheme would suffice. He castigated the project as a rash gamble, lacking proper professional advice, and as *only another way of getting people into the Arndale car parks*. Opponents of the scheme, who presumably by now were fully mobilised, could muster only 19 votes at the end of the meeting.

This was by no means the end of the frustrations for those supporting it. Dorset County Council deferred the planning application. It thought that a building of such size and importance needed a more spacious setting. The only way this could be achieved was to purchase and demolish five houses in Kingland Road. It was not an unreasonable request, but it would entail a compulsory purchase order. This was bound to increase costs and create further delay.

It also allowed objectors time to regroup and attack the scheme from other directions. Public sympathy might be aroused for those residents of Kingland Road whose homes were now threatened at the behest of the planning authority. There were also allegations that the public meeting in October 1972 had been misled about the Council's capital resources. It was said that they had been quoted as £820,000, compared with £792,000 at the meeting in April - and that in either case, the £430,000 cost of the new swimming baths should have been deducted. Colin Green, chairman of Poole Residents' Consultative Committee, demanded that Alderman Lloyd-Allen should resign as chairman of the Arts Centre sub-committee, if he did not reveal the contents of a secret report on the financial position.

Alderman Lloyd-Allen replied that the Council's capital position was already public knowledge. It held capital receipts totalling £1.26 million. After deducting the cost of the swimming baths and other minor schemes, there would in fact be £838,000 available for the Arts Centre project. Further capital receipts were anticipated before it was completed in 1976.

For all that, there were fears about financing the project. The Corporation stood to lose some of its powers, as a result of local government reform. Unless the scheme was finalised before changes in the law, some of its assets and cash balances might not be available. If earlier precedents were followed, they would be transferred to the authority which took over these powers from the Council. This might mean the loss of £100,000 in capital, as well as surplus land earmarked for sale or development. Another concern was whether the Western Orchestral Society would be able to meet its commitment of £175,000.

Acquisition of additional land for the Arts Centre and the grant of planning approval took most of 1973, but documents had been prepared in time for tenders to be received by the end of that year. Public excitement in anticipation of work commencing was at its height. It was time for the final decision. A large sum had already been provided for inflation, which showed no sign of abating. If it got worse, the Government might take draconian measures which could affect Poole's capital profits. On the other hand, the town's rateable value was rising, as more homes and offices were completed. If the Arts Centre was not started then, it might never be built. It would

Above: Bournemouth Symphony Orchestra performs in the Wessex Hall.
Below; The Towngate Theatre in Poole Arts Centre.

certainly be too much to expect the Council after 1974, with its reduced powers, and new members and officers, to undertake such a venture in its early years.

Then there was the evidence of the Council's previous experience on large capital schemes. It had often confronted inflation and increasing costs, and found it wiser in the long term to go ahead and not be discouraged. Poole's momentous years had encompassed projects of benefit to trade, commerce, and industry. Many councillors felt that the old Corporation should round off the renascence of the town with an Arts Centre to benefit other aspects of community life.

Those who authorised the signing of the contract did so in the knowledge that the new Council might inherit some pitfalls. These were to arrive sooner, and in a more severe form, than even they had anticipated. The Government's attempts to curb inflation did nothing to halt the increasing cost of building the Arts Centre, but they brought about a substantial fall in the value of building land. The estimated final cost rose to £4.5 million, while land values fell so much that the Council decided to postpone all further sales on Canford Heath.

Thus the stage was set for a political and financial crisis to come upon the new Council late in 1975, when the District Auditor issued an interim report on the accounts of the old council in its final year of existence. A superficial study of the report was enough to arouse passions about the shape and pace of Poole's redevelopment, the viability of the Arts Centre project, the financial security of those who had invested money with the Council, and many other less relevant issues and grievances. Some otherwise responsible critics would not bother to look beyond the headlines before joining in the chorus of *We told you so*. Those who struggled to bring about Poole's rebirth would stand accused of arrogance and over-reaching themselves. They would find a particular irony in Burke's observation that it is an error to imagine that the loudest complainers for the public are the most anxious for its welfare.

These events, and how matters turned out in the longer term, are dealt with in a *Postscript* at the end of this volume.

UPTON HOUSE

Upton House continued in the news throughout the 1960s. At first it was in relation to the social activities of its occupants, Prince Carol and Princess Jeanne of Romania. They were invited to many functions in the town, including the Mayor's Reception. The Princess was in considerable demand to open fetes and bazaars, and even on commercial occasions, such as the opening of a store or the start of a new private housing estate.

Before long, the royal glitter faded, amid unkind gossip, stories of Upton House being used for sales promotions, and county court proceedings against the Prince by tradesmen. It was said that lengths of carpet were being sold to the public as surplus to their Highnesses' requirements, and that some of Princess Jeanne's floral arrangements for a refurbished Bournemouth hotel featured onion plants which had gone to seed. She also tried to launch herself as an artist, painting portraits of local worthies from their photographs.

Princess Jeanne in conversation with King Hussein of Jordan.

All these things cast doubt upon the Council's hope that it had rid itself of the worry of maintenance and insurance for 16 years while the town grew out towards Upton House. Members demanded to be told if all the covenants regarding the lease had been observed, and if the rent was up to date. Because of the work that needed to be done to the house, the rent for the early years had been fixed at £2 a week. Opponents were able to accuse the Corporation having let a royal residence at no more than the rent of a council house!

More than once, just when it seemed that their affairs were at their lowest ebb, the Prince and Princess bounced back into the limelight in an unexpected fashion. The Princess made a trip to the Middle East, on which she met a number of religious leaders. Among the photographs was one taken by the official photographer to King Hussein of Jordan. It showed the King and the Princess seated next to each other in somewhat modest surroundings, taking part in discussions about a charitable project. Publication of the photograph in the local press seemed to imply that the Prince and Princess were of more standing and substance than recent events tended to suggest.

This publicity was as nothing to that which descended upon them in July 1965, when Ronald Biggs, one of the Great Train Robbers, escaped from Wandsworth Gaol. Biggs was reported to have been seen in the vicinity of Winterfold House, in Cranleigh, Surrey. Police carried out a fruitless search. Knowing what they did about affairs at Upton, many Poole people were mildly astonished by newspaper reports that Prince Carol was involved in negotiations to buy Winterfold House. A bigger surprise lay only a matter of twenty-four hours away. Poole police received a tip that Biggs had been seen in the grounds of Upton House.

The coincidence of the two reports was remarkable, and Dorset Police were bound to take the matter seriously. Biggs at one time lived at Swanage, and had appeared at Poole Quarter Sessions some eight years previously. On Saturday July 10, 1965, Upton House was surrounded by 100 police officers, some of them armed.

The search was commanded by Arthur Hambleton, the Chief Constable of Dorset, and included dog handlers, a contingent from Bournemouth Police, a Naval helicopter and Royal Marines assault craft. Again, no trace of Biggs was discovered.

The publicity that resulted for Prince Carol was considerable, but not quite the sort he could appreciate. 'Many people, reading about these two searches, will jump to the conclusion that there must be some other connection, which of course there is not,' he said. He thought the call about Upton House was a hoax from beginning to end.

The Prince's protestation of complete innocence of any involvement with Biggs was only finally settled when the Home Secretary announced in Parliament that Prince Carol was not suspected of being concerned with the Great Train Robbery. Despite the attention focused on Winterfold and Upton House, there was no such connection, be said.

His name may have been cleared, but Prince Carol's difficulty in paying his bills continued unabated. In 1967 the council issued a writ for the recovery of rent and the insurance premium. In 1968, be was summoned for non-payment of rates. Despite this, Prince Carol continued to press the Council to sell him the property. He told the Town Clerk his trustees would agree to let him use his capital for such a purchase, even though his income was rather restricted. He said that, if he owned the house, he could establish it as the headquarters of the Order of Knights of St John which would add to the prestige of the town. The Town Clerk took a sceptical view of the suggestion and took no action on it.

By February 1969, the council's patience was exhausted. Alderman Leslie Miller claimed that Upton House was 'falling to pieces' and that members of the Llewellin family, who presented it to the borough in 1957, were bitterly disappointed. Alderman Fred Rowe said the tenants had carried out the minimum of repairs. Bob Cass, the deputy Town Clerk, felt Upton House could fall into a worse state if it was left empty.

The last ironic twist of the saga was in June, 1969, when the Town Clerk received an invitation from *La Grande-Maitre de l'Ordre Souverain de St Jean de Jerusalem, Chevaliers de Malte - OSJ* to participate in the *ceremonie d'intronisation de Son Altesse Royale Carol, Prince de Roumanie comme le soixante-treizieme Grand Maitre de cet Ordre* at the Binnehauf à La Haye. The dress was *Uniformes ou Grand Gala*.

This grand occasion in the annals of chivalry attracted less local attention than the announcement, four months later, that Prince Carol would formally surrender his lease on December 31, and that the Council would waive its outstanding claims against him for rent, rates, insurance premiums and dilapidations. There were angry protests that this was tantamount to a farewell present, and that the Prince should receive the same treatment as other Council tenants. Horace Medway, chairman of the Housing Committee, was more pragmatic. He told the Council that they were only *making a present of something which we never had and which I feel we may never get.*

The Council was again in possession of its property. In January 1970, members were able to look round the house and grounds, when a tour of inspection was organised for the Planning Committee. Some felt the house was in a better state than they had been led to believe. Many were impressed by its atmosphere, and the potential of its attractive setting. Alderman Ron Hart complained that parts of the property *were really a right royal slum*, and did not think the Council could afford to restore it.

New offers for a tenancy were received, and pressure grew for the house and grounds to be opened to the public. The Council was adamant that this could not be done until there was a safe access on to the main road. This, in turn, would have to await completion of the Upton bypass, which was due in 1973.

BROWNSEA ISLAND

Brownsea Island recovered from its 1963 fire sufficiently well to be opened to the public again in 1964 and, that year, attracted 51,000 visitors. The same year, with Geoffrey Adams as Chairman, Brownsea Open Air Theatre was founded. An

The Boy Scout movement celebrated the sixtieth anniversary of its foundation on Brownsea Island with a national patrol leaders' camp in 1967.

amphitheatre was constructed in a field near St Mary's Church. Bournemouth Little Theatre Club presented *The Tempest* on three evenings in August. The 'man-eating mosquitoes,' however, continued to be quite a serious nuisance to visitors. Dorset Naturalists' Trust obtained a grant from the Nature Conservancy for a two-year study of the problem by an entomologist. He believed that the Brownsea mosquitoes were among the most vicious of 36 varieties found in the British Isles. The nuisance was never finally eradicated as many of the insects were bred in the marshes at the other side of the harbour.

The Boy Scout movement celebrated the diamond jubilee of its foundation on Brownsea with a national patrol leaders' camp on the island from July 29 to August 5, 1967. More than 250 patrol leaders from all parts of the United Kingdom, Europe and Africa were chosen to take part. It commenced 60 years to the day after Sir Robert Baden-Powell and a party of young men arrived on Brownsea for an experimental camp, to try out his ideas on character training and citizenship. Baden-Powell's daughter, the Hon Mrs Betty Clay, unveiled a stone commemorating the site of the first Scout camp in 1907.

COMPTON ACRES

The gardens at Compton Acres were first laid out between 1920 and 1923 but had fallen into neglect during the war. In 1950 they were bought by J Stanley Beard, a retired architect, who restored the seven gardens, and opened them to the public. They were attracting 75,000 visitors a year by 1963, when Mr Beard wished to retire. He offered the gardens to the Corporation, which declined to buy them. In December, 1963, he sold them to John Brady, subject to the covenant that if within seven years from Mr Beard's death the purchaser wished to sell, the gardens should first be offered to the Corporation.

PARKS AND OPEN SPACES

News of Poole Borough Council's major projects tended to eclipse the important, day-to-day work of its Committees, particularly the Culture and Recreation Committee (formerly the Parks Committee).

Since the war the Committee had greatly increased the area of the town's open spaces. The Corporation's refuse tip at Whitecliff had been converted into a recreation ground; a playing field had been established at Plainfield Farm with heathland connecting it to Broadstone Recreation Ground. Turlin Moor, a tidal swamp, had been converted into 82 acres of dry land, providing playing fields. Other recreation grounds had been created at Haskells, Tatnam Farm and Alderney, all with modern dressing rooms, as well as many smaller amenity areas and children's playgrounds.

Poole Park remained the area of open space that was central to the concerns of the Corporation and the public. Many decisions affecting it were generally welcomed. The

The mansion in the grounds of Compton Acres, later demolished to make way for a luxury flat development.

expense of installing a new sluice gate, to allow the water in the salt water lake to be changed more regularly, was one of them. It helped to obviate the swarms of midges which bred in the lake. Many new types of water fowl were introduced to the fresh water lakes, and in 1972-73 'Plant a Tree Year' was held, to encourage private planting of trees.

Though the amount of through traffic in the park tended to increase in proportion to that on main roads, it was still seen as something of a refuge from the motor vehicle. Its value in that role must have increased in 1964, when the Roads and Engineering Committee estimated that traffic in Poole would increase two and three-quarter times by 1989. Its plans to deal with the increase included a road to take traffic to the lower part of Poole, or to the new shopping centre, which would relieve the George roundabout. Of three suggested ways to accomplish this, and by far be cheapest was a new road through the side of Poole Park.

The Culture and Recreation Committee was prepared to consider the plan seriously. The salt water lake had been formed from the 54 acres of Parkstone Bay enclosed by the railway embankment. The lake, the ownership of which was in doubt, was considered inviolate when the park was constructed. With the great increase of population since then, some felt the lake was now too large in comparison with the

Poole Park, 1967.

much smaller land area. Reclaiming nine acres would provide new land to improve the park's amenities.

Public interest in the proposals was obviously very great. A petition against any proposals affecting the park was signed by 27,000 people, and stickers demanding 'Hands off Poole Park' were distributed. At a most vociferous and well-attended public meeting in 1965, consideration of the new road proposals was completely dominated by consideration of those affecting the park. Many alternative schemes were put forward, amid great suspicion that there were other secret plans affecting the park. The only proposal for the park upon which opinions differed was the tentative suggestion of the Culture and Recreation Committee that all through traffic might be banned.

The Roads and Engineering Committee quietly dropped its proposal to build the new road through the edge of the park and adopted the more expensive alternative of widening Mount Pleasant Road. A roundabout was constructed in Parkstone Road at the junction with Mount Pleasant Road. This development required the land to be raised, and the loss of a small portion of the park at Norton's Gate. This entrance to the park had to be closed to vehicles, and reconstructed to allow only pedestrian access. Landscaping was carried out to retain the character of the park.

Value for Money was the theme of this exhibition staged in Poole Park by local members of the National and Local Government Officers' Association.

THE SWAN LAKE CAFE

Antony Forte was granted the first concession to run the new Swan Lake Cafe in Poole Park. It was expected that it would be exempt from paying rates, as the previous cafe had been. The Corporation had successfully argued that the cafe was part of the amenities for people using the park, and that any profit from it should be offset against the expenses of providing the park.

On the assumption that this freedom from rates would continue, and to try to calm the political arguments in the Council about the policy of the cafe being operated by private enterprise, a high rental had been negotiated.

Mr Forte provided a lavishly furnished grill room in one third of the building, with a self-service cafe in the rest. A grand opening ceremony was arranged and the grill room was extensively advertised as a restaurant. It was this which undermined its exemption from rates. Patrons were invited to come and eat in the grill room, quite separately from visiting the park. The restaurant was open in the evening, when most of the park's other amenities had closed for the day. Eating there could no longer be regarded as ancillary to use of the park. Mr Forte lost his appeal and the Swan Lake became subject to rates.

With this extra burden, despite all Mr Forte's efforts, the cafe became unprofitable, and, in 1966 he applied to the Corporation for a revision of his lease, and for agreement to closing the grill room. The Committee refused to consider any amendment of the terms of the lease that included the closure of the grill room. Banquets of Oxford Ltd, already the lessees of the beach cafes and kiosks, took over the lease. In 1968, that company negotiated a revision of the terms whereby the whole cafe, including the grill room, could be made available for evening functions, but daytime usage of the grill room would be maintained for 12 months from June, 1968. After receiving the financial results for the grill room over that period, the Council reluctantly agreed that it could be discontinued and the area included in the cafe.

THE BEACHES, THEIR CAFES AND KIOSKS

Forte's Catering, which had operated the beach cafes and most of the kiosks on Poole's beaches for 14 years, was not successful in tendering for a new lease in 1964. This was won by Banquets of Oxford Ltd, a company formed by George Silver, a man whose enormous frame and completely bald head belied his pleasant nature.

Mr Silver established his catering business after an adventurous life with the 14th Army. He had great plans for the development of the Sandbanks restaurants and kiosks. These included a public house which, be claimed was very necessary. His staff were being asked over 70 times a day where visitors could get a drink. Some members of the council were enthusiastic supporters of the scheme but others wondered how a public house might affect the family attractions of Sandbanks. The Council decided not to support such a scheme and to rely, when it could be done, on a general improvement of the existing facilities.

Though there were many improvements to beach huts
and promenades, wooden huts gave a pre-war quality
to the seafront at Canford Cliffs Chine.

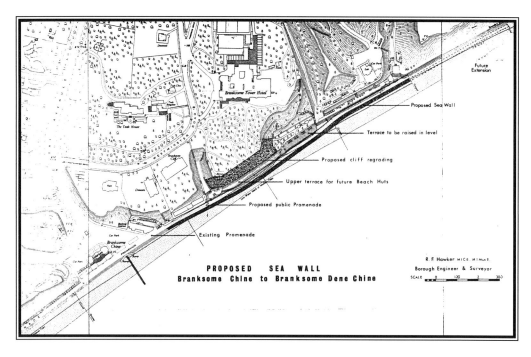

Top: Reluctance on the part of some landowners delayed the plan to complete one of the missing links in Poole's seafront promenades – the section between Branksome Chine and Branksome Dene Chine.
Below: Installing the "GW" cliff stabilisation system at Canford Cliffs.

Throughout the period the Council continued its policy of providing permanent beach chalets on the promenades of its beaches. Its policy of letting these chalets to residents who had the right to sublet them for short periods each year, was maintained. A few were let to visitors on a weekly basis, and to clubs, charities and the hotels association. By 1973 well over 1,000 chalets had been provided at rentals of up to £52 a year.

The construction of the promenades, stretching from Shore Road to the borough boundary, and the protection of the cliffs, were the responsibility of the Borough Engineer and his staff. Promenades were built when sea defences were brought up to date. As part of this work most of the cliffs behind the promenades were made stable by cutting them back to an 'angle of repose.'

This, though, was not possible in the case of the cliffs at Canford Cliffs where Cliff Drive ran along the side and near to the top of the cliff. Here, Lionel Gregory, a Poole architect, and Arthur White, Assistant Borough Engineer, devised a new system of cliff stabilisation. Their 'GW' system would support the cliff at a considerably steeper angle and without spoiling the natural beauty of the area. The commentator in a BBC programme, devoted to the work, described the system succinctly:

The method they have come up with is surprisingly simple. It consists of a giant rope ladder, and this rope ladder, instead of supporting people, is going to support the cliff face. Long cables are strung down the side of the cliff, but like all rope ladders, success depends on getting strong support at the top. To be absolutely sure of firm ground meant going back 20 feet from the cliff edge, well back into the main road. In a trench each individual strand of wire in the cable is connected to a 'T' shaped frame. When the top is secure, the cable is tightened at the foot of the cliff to remove any slack.

At regular intervals down the plastic covered cable, cradles made out of galvanised mild steel are bolted, and this cradle will support the rungs of the ladder. The rungs are enormous troughs – giant window boxes, if you like – and this whole construction has got to be pretty sturdily put together because, if it is going to work, this arrangement has got to last not for one year or two, but for one generation or two.

The new cliff face was formed, hiding the 104 steel troughs, and finally sprayed with a mixture of grass seed, wood pulp, fertiliser and resin.

SWIMMING BATH

With hindsight it seems more than a little surprising that it took Poole so long to acquire a public swimming bath that could unequivocally be said to be worthy of the borough. The argument often heard was that there was no need for one, when Poole was a seaside town. The line of reasoning usually stopped there, when, for that selfsame reason, there was a greater need for people to learn to swim in safe surroundings.

The reluctance of the Council to provide a swimming bath was deeply entrenched, as Herbert Carter, a Freeman and former Mayor, could testify. He wrote, in his book *I Call to Mind:* 'Just before the Municipal Elections in November, 1908, a resolution was passed by the Council that Swimming Baths should be provided on a site near the Salt

Water Lake in Poole Park. The resolution was "at long last," for I remembered being shown a scheme fifteen years before which Mr Elford, the Borough Engineer, had been directed to prepare.'

It took the Council about a quarter of a century to produce an open air swimming bath in Park Lake Road. Its modest amenities were overlooked by a railway line and a gasworks. It was still in occasional use in the summer of 1961 when the Council resolved to build new indoor baths as part of the Civic Centre site. It purchased The Knoll and Moorcroft, two large houses on the corner of Commercial Road and Park Road, for the site, despite the persistent predictions of Alderman Arthur Butler that the baths would never be built there.

Two years later, the Parks Committee put forward plans to erect the baths, estimated to cost £300,000, but the general opinion of the council was that it was a luxury which the borough could not afford.

In the end, Alderman Butler's prophecy came true, thanks in part to the Borough Architect looking into the future himself. Defeat in the Council gave the Parks Committee time for further thought. It decided that a site near the Arndale Centre would be much more appropriate, and the Council agreed. The committee put forward a new scheme at a cost of £300,000 and suggested that there could be no more appropriate use of capital profits made by the council.

The site for the baths at first seemed an extraordinary one. It was north of the old Grammar School buildings in Kingland Road, and partly hidden by them. The Borough Architect explained that the Education Committee planned to close the school premises, which had become Seldown Secondary School. There would be a need for another bridge over the railway at this point, to give access to the eastern side of the Old Town. When this had been done, choice of site for the baths, and a car park, would be seen to be justified.

The Council was in a much stronger financial position in 1969 when the Parks Committee brought forward new plans at an estimated cost of £435,000. It felt that it could reasonably afford to provide this amenity, even though there would be a charge on the rates for its running expenses.

Because of severe Government restrictions on capital projects, the Council's loan application was deferred, even though it obtained a Category A rating among schemes submitted to the Western Sports Council. Early in 1970, when other local authorities had been unable to meet the time limits for taking up loan sanctions, the Ministry cancelled them and gave the council its approval.

The plans showed a main pool 33.33 metres long by 12.5 metres wide, with adjoining teaching and diving pools. Building was to begin in 1970 with completion in 1973, but the contract was beset with problems. Brick shortages led to delays; craftsmen went on strike for higher wages, and the shifting sand of the subsoil required extra work to stabilise it. It was a great disappointment to the Council that the baths were not opened until after the old Borough Council had been succeeded by the new Poole District Council.

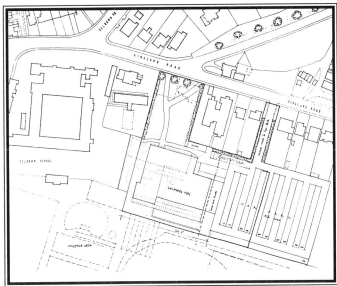

Top: The Dolphin swimming pool.

Left: The choice of site for the indoor swimming bath took account of future developments, such as demolition of the old Grammar School buildings and the construction of Seldown Bridge.

Something of an end-of-term feeling may have developed in local town halls as the reforms of 1974 arrived, but in Poole it was tinged with sadness that the old Council was not able to oversee all its schemes to fruition.

THE STATUS OF THE TOWN

In 1963 the Council was still waiting impatiently for the Minister's promised proposals for the review of local government. He had promised this in 1955 when he effectively blocked the Corporation's private Bill to constitute Poole a county borough, a status which had been proposed by the Boundary Commission as early as 1947.

It was, though, not until March 1958, that Parliament eventually passed the Local Government Act. This set up another Commission, the Local Government Commission, to recommend a new system of local government.

By this time the Council was encouraged to learn that the two first criteria which the commission was asked to bear in mind were the community of interests of an area and its expected developments. The Council believed that its case for county borough status had been greatly boosted by the South-East Study, established by the Government to assess the region's land requirements. It had concluded that Poole was a suitable area for expansion of 20,000 population in the following twenty years, bringing its population in 1981 up to 120,000.

However, despite the eloquent plea of Sir Richard Pilkington, its Member of Parliament, for early consideration of Poole's case, the Commission first turned its attention to the northern areas of the country. It was 1965 before it began its review of the south by asking local authorities to answer a questionnaire and make proposals, and the whole sorry business of inevitable conflict between the various local government authorities began once more.

Poole's only territorial demand was that the anomaly of Brownsea Island and other islands of the harbour being excluded from the town's boundaries should be corrected. Without making any definite claim, it suggested that the Commission should consider whether Corfe Mullen and parts of Upton should form part of the borough.

Not unnaturally, with Poole residents contributing so much in rates, Dorset County Council opposed the Council's proposals. Bournemouth Council proposed amalgamation with most of Poole, and the Wimborne councils proposed that, if Poole was granted county borough status, Canford and Merley should be excluded.

In November 1965, representatives of the Council were invited to London to discuss Poole's proposals. When the Conservative Aldermen Lloyd-Allen and Miss Bisgood, the Liberal Alderman Ballam and the Labour Alderman Mrs Hickinson, attended this meeting, there were already rumours that the future of the Commission was in doubt. When Sir Harry Hancock, chairman of the Commission, resigned,

Councillor Rhodam Hewitt   *Councillor Stanley Pearce*

followed by his vice-chairman, Sir Michael Rowe, and Professor Ely Devons, the rumours seemed confirmed.

The Council, believing in its case, was alarmed by these developments and wrote to the Commission and to Richard Crossman, the Minister. It pointed out that, if the Council's claim was aborted, it would be the third time this had happened in the previous twenty years and asked that, in the interests of effective local government, the Commission's recommendations in regard to the area should be implemented.

Poole's plea was in vain. In February 1966, the Government abolished the Local Government Commission and announced the setting up of a Royal Commission to make recommendations for the reform of local government. The Minister denied that the setting up of a Royal Commission was a ploy to avoid difficult decisions. With all the information available to the Commission, the Minister believed that the Commission's report could be prepared in two years, to which statutory effect could quickly be given.

Sir John Maud was appointed the chairman of the Royal Commission, which consisted of eleven appointees by the Government. Again, the Corporation was asked to submit evidence, as were 58 county councils, 34 London boroughs, 58 county boroughs, 270 boroughs, 538 Urban District Councils, 473 Rural District Councils, and 7,300 parish councils. In a later survey it was reported that one-third of councils consulted supported a regional system in which local government functions were delegated to eight or nine regional councils. A third supported the 'City Regional' concept of large, 'free-standing' towns and conurbations which had a community of

Councillor Peter Horner   Councillor Kevin Chaffey

interest. The rest supported the existing 'two-tier' system or a two-tier system based on a 'city regions' or 'continuous county' system.

It was, though, not until July 1969, that the Commission issued its majority report. It recommended the setting up of eight Provincial Councils, each to settle the framework of its area and plan educational, recreational and personal services. In these eight regions, there were to be 58 'all-purpose' unitary authorities,

Poole was to be included in 'Unit 40' within the proposed South-West Province. This 'all purpose' authority was to be based on Bournemouth and include Poole, the county of Dorset, Christchurch, Lymington and Fordingbridge.

The Government invited local authorities to comment on the recommendations of the Royal Commission. Poole prepared a detailed criticism, the main thrust of which was that it still was of the opinion that reform should be based on areas with which people clearly identified themselves, rather than arbitrarily defined ones.

The Association of Municipal Corporations produced a detailed alternative plan which it submitted to regional conferences. It proposed the formation of 13 Provincial and 132 'most purpose' authorities, one of them being Poole. Its 'Wessex Province', one of the provinces suggested, included Hampshire, the Isle of Wight, the county of Dorset and the southern part of Wiltshire, an area which would have a rateable value of £93m. The Labour Government, however, was still heavily engaged in battling against economic problems. In 1969 it suffered a humiliating defeat by its own backbenchers and the trade unions, and was forced to abandon plans to curb unofficial strikes. Before it could come to any conclusion on the recommendations of the Royal Commission, the

Stanley Milburn, Deputy Borough Treasurer

Leslie Scrase, Parks Superintendent

Government was defeated in the 1970 General Election by the Conservative Party under Edward Heath.

Peter Walker, the new Minister responsible for local government, had his own ideas on what reforms could be quickly achieved. He rejected the idea of establishing Provinces incorporating a number of 'all purpose' authorities. He decided to set up unelected bodies to take over most of the health duties of local authorities, as well as the responsibility for the provision of water services, sewerage and sewage disposal duties. He rejected the proposal for regional provinces for local authorities. Otherwise, he adopted the suggestion of the County Councils Association that the county councils should be the major authority for local services, with 'District Councils' dealing with some of the minor, more local duties, such as housing, refuse collection, museums, planning, parks and the maintenance of minor urban roads.

It was a severe blow to the members of the Poole Council who had battled for so many years for more powers and to be free of all involvement with the county council. It was no comfort to them that its old adversary, the county borough of Bournemouth, had lost even more powers, for it, too, was to be demoted to a District Council.

The Council continued to fight for what it believed to be its due, but the Minister brushed all opposition to his plan aside, and set a time-table on which the various stages of the transition should take place. Elections to the new councils were to take place in April, 1973, and the new authorities would come into operation on 1 April, 1974. New regional Health Authorities and Water Boards were to come into operation before that date. The Acts embodying these changes were duly passed by Parliament after many hours of debate, and the Council had no alternative but to make the best of what it considered to be a bad system.

There was, however, much work to be done to complete the plans which the Council had in hand. It still hoped to complete the swimming bath, despite strikes by the workers and the shortage of bricks. It would be left to the new council to see the completion of the Arts Centre and set up a management structure. The second stage of the Canford Heath development would be well under way, but would take many years to complete. In addition, the usual run of council business had to be carried on.

Some of the major interests of senior members of the Council would be transferred to the new county council. As a consequence, Jeanne Bisgood, chairman of Poole Committee for Education, did not stand for election to the new district council, but became chairman of Dorset County Council's Committee for Education. Similarly, Air Commodore McIntyre, chairman of Poole's Highways Committee, left to become a member of the county council, of which he later became chairman. Fred Rowe, chairman of Poole's Culture and Recreation Committee, concentrated his service in the county council, where be became the vice-chairman of its committee dealing with recreation services, for which be was awarded the OBE.

Many of the members of the Borough Council, however, did successfully stand for election to the new council. Arthur Lloyd-Allen became a councillor in the new Poole District Council, the office of Alderman having been abolished. He was elected chairman of its Policy and Resources Committee. Bob Hann became chairman of its Housing Committee, with Kevin Chaffey as its vice-chairman; Rhodam Hewitt became chairman of the new Planning and Highways Committee, with Peter Horner as his vice-chairman; Stanley Pearce became chairman of the Recreation Committee, with Adrian Greenwood as his vice-chairman. The new council, therefore, began with members with great experience in local affairs of the town.

The new council was not so successful in retaining the services of senior staff. The "Three H's" - as John Hillier, Bob Hawker and Geoffrey Hopkinson (respectively the Town Clerk, Borough Engineer and Borough Architect), became known in the Municipal Buildings from their regular Monday morning meetings to plan and co-ordinate the work of the council were all approaching retirement age. They decided to take early retirement. Stanley Milburn, the only other usual member of the Monday morning discussion, opted to transfer to the new council as Borough Treasurer. The welfare duties of the Medical Officer of Health, Dr James Hutton, had been transferred back to the county a year or so earlier. The post of Medical Officer of Health for Poole was abolished. He became an Area Medical Officer of the county. Bob Cass, the Deputy Town Clerk, left the Corporation to enter private practice. Arthur Ingham, the Borough Education Officer, retired on the office being abolished as the new county council took over all educational functions. Arthur White, the joint chief engineering assistant, left to become chief engineer to Wimborne Council. The only departmental head of the old council to be appointed to a similar position in the new county council was Geoffrey Roberts, who became the chief officer of its Trading Standards Department. With the responsibility for the town's parks remaining with the new Poole council, Leslie Scrase, the recently appointed officer, remained as Borough Amenities Officer.

There remained a wealth of experience in the remaining staff who transferred to the new Poole Council. Ian Andrews and Michael Wickenden, the two Assistant Town Clerks, were appointed Town Clerk and Chief Executive Officer and Deputy, respectively.

Albert Marsden, deputy Borough Engineer, was appointed Borough Engineer, and Graham Rogers, Deputy Borough Architect was appointed Borough Architect. Most of the important ancillary staffs of the various departments still remained in place.

The last members of the Borough and County of the Town of Poole and its chief officers decided to end their work together with the flourish. They treated themselves to a final dinner in the Conference Room of the Municipal Buildings. Those present at the dinner managed to make the event a happy one, even though they were conscious that they were celebrating the end of the Borough and County of the Town of Poole after more than 400 years of its existence. The speakers concentrated on their achievements. The only regrets expressed were that they had not been able to complete some of their projects.

The Mayor, on behalf of the members, presented the three retiring chief officers with generous parting gifts. The Town Clerk, on behalf of them, presented all members of the Council with a specially printed and bound copy of *The Pride of Poole*, a book specially written by Derek Beamish, a lecturer in local history, in collaboration with the Town Clerk and John Dockerill, the Museums Curator. It described events which took place in Poole following a previous reform of local government in 1835. It was this book, published by the Corporation in soft covers, that became a popular success and led to the formation of Poole Historical Trust.

All present joined in wishing the new council well. The old Council's only other regret was that it had not achieved a better outcome in its fight for autonomy. There was then nothing to do but to say their final goodbyes, and leave the scene to others.

SOME OF THE PEOPLE OF POOLE

ANDREWS, Arthur H. Principal of Poole Technical College, died suddenly aged 60 in June, 1966. Trained at the Royal College of Art, he was one of the few artists to hold such a position. Came to Poole in 1947, when he was appointed to reorganise facilities for technical and further education in east Dorset, which then consisted of a small school of art and an evening institute, with four full-time and 400 part-time students. He saw the college roll grow to several thousand full and part time students, and was instrumental in building up its art collection.

Herbert Ballam

BALLAM, Herbert Charles Richard, a long serving Liberal member of Poole Borough Council, to which he was first elected in 1949. He served as Sheriff in 1962/63, Mayor in 1963/64 and was elected Alderman during his year of office. He continued to serve as a member of the new District Council of Poole from 1974. He was Liberal candidate for Poole in the 1964 General Election, and the fourth generation of his family to serve on the borough or county council. Described by the *Poole and Dorset Herald* as 'a hard worker who places politics a long way second to principle...the ideal man for a councillor.'

BENSON, Sir Christopher, succeeded Geoffrey Fenn as negotiator for Arndale Developments Ltd in 1964. When, in 1969, the company was taken over by the Town & City company, he established Dolphin Developments Ltd in Poole and took the old Dolphin Brewery's design of a dolphin as its symbol. During the appeal for funds for the Sports Centre he piloted his helicopter to Poole to help. He then joined Law Land, as an assistant managing director, and shortly afterwards was appointed managing director, a position he held till 1988. He is, or has been, managing director or chairman of many public companies, including Sun Alliance Group, MEP, Boots, House of Fraser, Albright & Wilson, as well as a director of a number of national charities. He was knighted in 1988.

BLACKBURN, Tony, the son of a Lilliput family doctor, was at the age of 22 in 1965 the most popular disc jockey on board the 'pirate' radio ship, Radio Caroline, moored about three miles off the Essex coast. He received more than 100 fan letters a day.

BROWN, George ('Jojo'), of Ballard Road, Poole, retired in 1965, aged 65, after 40 years as a Trinity House pilot in Poole. It marked the end of three generations of service as pilots, totalling more than 200 years, by Mr Brown, his father, grandfather and two uncles. Mr Brown became the youngest Trinity House pilot in the country at the age of 24. In June 1940 he was the only survivor from a Dutch vessel which struck a magnetic mine near Hook Sands.

Mary Campbell

CAMPBELL, Mary. Born at Christchurch, she was one of the first residents of Chaddesley Glen, Canford Cliffs. Her father built a house there on his retirement in 1918, when it was little more than a woodland track. She retired from her teaching career in 1962 as deputy head of Saint Walburga's School, Bournemouth, and was secretary of Dorset Caledonian Society. Her wide circle of friends ranged from hotel workers to senior officers of Dorset Police. She died in 1974, aged 73.

CHIPPENDALE. Samuel. A small man with a pronounced North Country accent who established the Arndale Development Company in Bradford. The company thrived and became a national developer. It was 'Sam' Chippendale who first promoted the provision of under-cover malls as the future shape of shopping. His experience of seeing the deterioration of the centres of towns in America, as out-of-town shopping grew, led him to exhort the Government to take action to restrict such developments before the same thing happened here. His campaign was ignored until recent times. Meanwhile, the Arndale company over-reached its financial resources, and the unfortunate Mr Chippendale was forced to agree to his company being taken over by Town & City Properties. It was, though, not before other Arndale Centres had been commenced at Stretford, Nelson, Leeds, Doncaster, Manchester, Wandsworth and Luton.

CHURCHILL, Sir Winston, who joined Poole's illustrious line of Honorary Freemen in 1954, died in 1965. The Mayor and Town Clerk were invited to represent the town at the Memorial Service at St Paul's Cathedral, London. The town held its own civic memorial service at St James' Parish Church, Poole.

COOPER, Garry, aged 20, a steel erector, suffered severe burns to his arms and legs when he attempted to rescue three young children who died in a fire in an attic at the Old Town Cafe, High Street, in June 1965. He was awarded the British Empire Medal. Admirers from all parts of the country subscribed £200 in recognition of his bravery, which was presented to him by the Mayor.

DINGWALL, Mrs Louisa Lilian ('Ringo') (?1890-1982). An early feminist who served as a despatch rider and ambulance driver during the first world war. Better known for many years by her maiden name of Miss Foott, she ran a garage at Sandbanks, from which she provided Poole with its first bus service, with converted Model 'T' Fords. Her first bus she christened 'Henry', and the following ones were named 'Henry II', and so on until 'Henry VIII,' when she began naming them after Henry VIII's wives. After 'Anne Boleyn' she began a more conventional service with yellow-painted buses in Upper Parkstone. Her Rossmore Bus Company clung defiantly to its routes in the face of competition from the much larger Hants and Dorset Motor Services. It was eventually sold to Cosy Coaches of Parkstone, who continued to operate *The Monkey's Hump and Heavenly Bottom Express*. She also trained racehorses at Sandbanks, exercising them on the beach. Between 1948 and 1979 she saddled 41 flat and 28 National Hunt winners, as well as three in French races. Because of the racing establishment's opposition to women trainers she was obliged to make entries in the name of her stable lad, Charlie Pratt. At Brighton races in 1965 the Duke of Norfolk ordered her out of the weighing room. 'Women are banned,' be explained. 'I would have asked my wife to leave.' He later apologised to Mrs Dingwall, who described the Duke's action as 'silly and petty.' After she had been training horses for 34 years, women eventually won the right to be officially recognised as trainers.

DOMINEY, Reginald. Rose from office boy to director and general manager of John J Norton and Son, timber importers, from which he retired in 1972, aged 65. The business was founded in Poole in 1872. He was the last employee to be taken on personally by the founder, John J Norton, in 1922. He did not receive a wage of 7s 6d [37.5p] a week until he had spent a month working 'on trial.' At the end of a four-year apprenticeship, his pay had risen to 15s [75p]. Mr Norton's apprentices were not allowed to marry or gamble; smoking was strongly discouraged; and at the end of their apprenticeship, they had to make up periods of sick leave by working an equivalent time at the wages they were earning when they were away from work!

DOMINY, Harold. Spent practically all his working life in Poole as a carpenter and joiner. Worked 21 years for Rawlings (Builders) Ltd, West Quay Road. When he retired, aged 65, in 1971, he revealed that he had signed his name on many examples of his craftsmanship. He had also noted down dates and rates of pay, and tucked pages from newspapers of the day inside flush doors before finishing them.

DRUDGE, George Frederick Leslie, was elected to Poole Council in 1953; elected Sheriff in 1963, and Mayor in 1965. He was made an MBE in 1965 for his work for the welfare of ex-servicemen. Born in 1891, he was one of the first 50 members of the Royal Flying Corps when it was formed in 1912, and in 1963 he launched a reunion club for the 'stringbag' veterans of the first world war.

FABRICIUS, Jan, doyen of Dutch dramatists, came to live in Poole in 1938. The author of more than 20 plays, he was a household name in Holland, being known as the 'flower of Dutch literature.' He lived at Caesar's Camp, in Roman Road, Broadstone. He took British nationality in 1950, and on his 90th birthday was presented with a specially struck medal by representatives of Dutch cultural life. He died in 1964, aged 93. At the funeral service in St John's Church, Broadstone, the Queen of Holland, and the headmaster of the Jan Fabricius School, were represented by the burgomaster of his home town of Assen.

FRATER, Edward Charles, came back to England from Czechoslovakia with Mr K Guttenstein and others in 1937 to establish Loewy Engineering Company in Branksome Park. 'Eddie' Frater masterminded the erection of the company's new premises in Wallisdown Road and houses for its employees in Loewy Crescent. The company was taken over by Tube Investments in 1960. He was a great supporter of local business associations as well as the council's projects.

Ernest Gale

Councillor Dennis Gooding

GALE, Ernest W B, a Fellow of the Institute of Parks Administration who, after extensive experience as Parks Superintendent at Southall and Slough, was appointed Superintendent of Parks, Cemeteries and Allotments in Poole in 1950. He was involved in the Institute of Parks Administration for many years, becoming its President in 1962, but was best known in Poole as Secretary of the Poole Show. He retired in 1972 and was succeeded by Mr L G Scrase, also from Slough.

GOODING, Denis. A Labour member of the Council from 1963, who became Sheriff in 1971/72 and Mayor 1975/76. For many years worked in Poole for the Dorset ambulance service, and was, with his wife, an enthusiastic supporter of the Boy Scout and Girl Guide movements.

GREENWOOD, Bland Adrian. Born 1932, a solicitor, he was in 1961 the youngest member of Poole Borough Council when first elected as a Conservative for Parkstone ward, which he continued to represent on the new district council from 1974. Sheriff of Poole, 1967/68, Alderman 1970, Mayor 1971/72, and 1996/97.

HANN, Robert. A Poole councillor from 1954 until 1974, he was affectionately known as 'the Mayor of Broadstone.' He had been a member of the Royal Army Medical Corps from 1926 until 1945, when he established a taxi service in Broadstone. He refused the Council's offer to elect him as an Alderman, saying that, as opposed to the people of Broadstone, he did not trust a future council to re-elect him at the end of his term of office. He was Sheriff 1965/66 and Mayor 1968/69. For ten years he was a member, and latterly Chairman, of St Leonard's and Douglas House Hospitals. He was Chairman of Poole and East Dorset Water Board before it was dissolved in 1974.

HICKINSON, Mrs Elsie May, Freeman of Poole. Born 1901 in Victoria Road, Parkstone, into a family of 12 children, she joined the Labour Party in 1928, became a magistrate in 1942, and a borough councillor in 1945. She was Sheriff in 1958/59 and became only the second woman Mayor of Poole in 1961/62. She was the longest serving member of the Borough Council when it was abolished in 1974, and was looked upon as providing the touchstone of local opinion. In 1970, when she had served 25 years, her colleagues and the chief officers presented her with a gold watch. She was chairman of the Libraries Committee, and also served as a governor or manager of many local

Alderman Mrs Hickinson and Bernard Short

schools - including Saint Peter's Church School, Parkstone, which she left at 13 to become a baby minder at a weekly wage of 2s 6d [12.5p]. The Council unanimously decided in June, 1970, to offer Mrs Hickinson and Alderman Lloyd-Allen the Honorary Freedom of the Borough.

HUTCHINSON, Alan Clifford. Succeeded Arthur H Andrews as Principal of Poole Technical College in 1966. Born in Southampton, he was an evacuee in Poole for three years during the second world war. By developing an ambitious programme of arts and cultural events at the College, he did a great deal to rally support for the building of an Arts Centre for the town. There is no doubt that he would have continued to make a major contribution to community life had he not, on the casting vote of the chairman of the selection committee, failed to be appointed as the first principal of the combined Bournemouth and Poole Technical College. His departure was a great loss to the town.

LE CARRÉ, John, nom-de-plume of David John Moore Cornwell, who was born in Poole in 1931, and grew up at the family home in Mount Road, Parkstone. He was the grandson of Alderman A E J Cornwell, who was Mayor of Poole in 1928. His father, R T A ('Ronnie') Cornwell, who had a colourful business career of varying fortunes, was one of the founders of Poole Round Table No. 12. Working in the British Consulate in Hamburg in 1954 David Cornwell wrote *The Spy Who Came In From the Cold* (published in 1963), for which be adopted pseudonym of le Carré.

Air Commodore K J McIntyre

LENNON, John, of Beatles fame, in 1965, paid £25,000 for a six-bedroomed semi-bungalow with harbour frontage in Panorama Road, Sandbanks, for his Aunt Mimi to retire to, unmolested by souvenir-hunting fans who besieged her house in Liverpool. Her new home, overlooking the harbour mouth, was regularly pointed out to passengers on pleasure boat trips around the harbour.

McINTYRE, Air Commodore Kenneth John, CB, CBE, was elected as a Conservative borough councillor in 1966, and became a Poole magistrate in 1967. After training at Sandhurst, he was seconded from the Army to the Royal Air Force in 1934, and permanently transferred in 1945. He was director of staff at the Air Ministry when he retired in from the RAF in 1958.

MILLER, John William, a solicitor who was acting Town Clerk of Dorchester 1914-1919, Town Clerk of Wareham 1921-1936. Appointed clerk to Wareham Justices in 1935, he was believed to be the oldest magistrates' clerk still serving in British courts when he retired on his 85th birthday in 1963. He established a practice in Poole at Equity Chambers, High Street, and was appointed borough Coroner in 1929. He was the oldest serving Coroner in the country when he died in 1971, aged 93, and was succeeded as Coroner by his son.

MONTAGUE, Mrs Dorothy Irene (Rene). After two narrow failures she was elected to the Council as a Conservative in 1965, and quickly made her mark. She became chairman of the Health Committee after only two years' service; elected Alderman in 1970; Sheriff in 1971, and Mayor in 1973/74, the last year of the existence of the Borough Council. She later continued her service on the new Poole District Council, retiring in 1987.

MULES, Commander Nicholas Marwood ('Hank'). Appointed full-time Clerk and Chief Executive to Poole Harbour Commissioners in 1970, he became one of the most colourful characters of the port whose fortunes he set out to revive. In the process, he often crossed swords with the Borough Council on such issues as the Quay Hotel development, ownership of the quayside, and its conflicting roles as a working quay and tourist attraction. He oversaw reorganisation of the dock labour force, the start of freight ferry services to Cherbourg, and a major port expansion scheme at Hamworthy.

Oscar Murton

MURTON, Henry Oscar, OBE, TD (later Lord Murton of Lindisfarne). Born May 8, 1914, retired to Broadstone in 1957. He had been managing director of a company with department stores in Newcastle and Sunderland. Elected to Poole Borough Council 1961, JP 1963. In 1964, as Chairman of Poole Conservative Association, he was chosen as Parliamentary candidate, and during the election campaign set out to canvass every home in the borough personally. He was elected MP for Poole to succeed Sir Richard Pilkington, Conservative MP since 1951, who retired through ill health. He was secretary to the Conservative committee for housing and local government from 1964, and vice-chairman from 1967. In 1974 he became a senior Government whip, and was subsequently appointed Deputy Speaker of the House of Commons. It was widely believed that Mr Murton would have been chosen to succeed George Thomas as Speaker, but he cut short his Parliamentary career when his wife Constance, whom he married in 1939, became seriously ill. He was later given a life peerage.

ROCKLEY, Lord. His country house was at Lytchett Heath, Lytchett Minster. He owned Lytchett Heath and Ham Common, which included land at Rockley Point which he sold to the Corporation for the formation of Rockley Sands Holiday Camp. He was a director of National Provincial Bank, and a member of the Board responsible for the health services of the region from 1974.

ROWE, Frederick George, OBE, one of Poole Borough Council's most outspoken 'characters,' was a Conservative member of the Council from 1959 until 1985. A building contractor, he marked his debut in the Council chamber by protesting at the policy that members of his industry were not allowed to serve on the Planning Committee. He was elected to Dorset County Council in 1963 after a campaign in which he referred to the council as *a blood-sucking octopus* and to County Hall as *a gin palace*. He was chairman of the Borough Council's Culture and Recreation Committee 1961-1974, and chairman of Dorset Playing Fields Association for many years. He was elected Alderman and Mayor in 1967, and in 1972/73 was only the second member of the council to be elected Sheriff after serving as Mayor. With Alderman Haskins, he was a prime mover in the establishment of Poole Sports Centre. He owned a number of successful racehorses, among which was the winner of the Whitbread Cup, and a horse he named 'Poole Park,' which won a number of races.

SHERRIN, Thomas William ('Tom'), a jovial, kind-hearted man, the most swashbuckling of the many 'characters' who served on Poole Borough Council during the period. Born in Bournemouth in 1906, he was Sheriff in 1961/62, and was elected Mayor and Alderman in 1964. He was unselfconscious of his great size, weighing 24 stones, 12 lbs 11 oz in mayoral regalia. He attracted great publicity for Poole's resistance to being taken over by Bournemouth by sitting astride the gun barrel of a Churchill tank, which was placed by the Army in front of the Municipal Buildings as part of a recruiting campaign. He died in 1970.

SHORT, Bernard Charles, was appointed Borough Librarian and Museum Curator in 1919, after being librarian and secretary to Branksome Urban District Council from 1903 until it was merged with Poole. He wrote many books and articles on the history of Poole, and deserves be ranked alongside H P Smith as one of the town's most dedicated historians. He retired in 1955 and died in 1970.

SIEGER, Joshua. During the second world war he was a radar scientist at Worth Matravers in the Air Ministry Research Establishment. He was later involved in adapting radar equipment for use in aircraft for which the Air Ministry built a new factory in Francis Avenue, West Howe. After some years in the USA Mr Sieger returned to Britain and became managing director of Hamworthy Engineering, succeeding Sidney Hall, one of the founders of the business. In 1959, he founded J and S Sieger to make systems to detect and warn of the presence of poisonous gases. Production began at premises in Stanley Green Road, and later moved to the Nuffield Industrial Estate. The company prospered, exporting over 80 per cent of production. He was awarded the OBE for services to export. In 1967 he became Chairman of the Wessex Export Club, which was founded by Fred Rowe at the behest of the Ministry of Trade.

SILVER, George, formed his company, Banquets of Oxford, after war service in the Army Catering Corps. The company held the leases of Corporation cafes. His enormous size and completely bald head belied his charming and cheerful nature - so much so that a film director, seeing him in Oxford Street, London, persuaded him to accept a villain's part in a film he was making with Gina Lollobrigida as star. Afterwards he took a number of such supporting parts in further films.

STEPTOE, James, OBE, Clerk to Sturminster Rural Council for 26 years until retiring to Broadstone in 1960, was a member of Poole Borough Council for nine years until he resigned in 1973. He was elected an Alderman and Mayor in 1970, and succeeded Alderman Haskins as Chairman of the Planning Committee and as a member of the Planning Committee of the Association of Municipal Corporations.

STOKES, Albert John ('Bert'). An influential member of the Council from 1947, he was Sheriff in 1956, and elected Alderman and Mayor on the same day in 1959. His service was characterised by great love of his native town. He was a vigorous champion of Poole's tourist attractions and of the campaign to secure a Poole postal address for all parts of the borough. His outspoken stance on these issues was a cause of controversy when he called for Parkstone Grammar School to be renamed *Poole Grammar School for Girls* on its removal from Ashley Cross to new premises in Sopers Lane, Waterloo. He enlisted in the Royal Artillery at the age of 17, during the First World War, and won the Meritorious Service Medal for gallantry at the third battle of Ypres. He died in 1964, aged 68. His older brother, Charles, served on the council between 1937 and 1961, was Sheriff in 1952, Mayor in 1955, and died in 1962, aged 77.

TROTT, Miss Dorothy Amy. A Conservative member of the Council from 1967, becoming Sheriff in 1975. She wrote in her autobiography *A Tapestry of Life*: 'I must have been born in the early Spring of 1903, possibly in London, and although I have no proof of my parentage, rumour has it that my mother was an Italian opera singer at Covent Garden in 1901-1902 and my father probably the spoilt only son of a wealthy industrialist.' After being placed in an orphanage she was brought up by foster-parents. She lived most of her life in Yorkshire, where she was principal of three girls' schools. On selling them she retired to Branksome Park and drove a Rolls-Royce, which always seemed too large for her. Her experience with schools was put to good use as a member

Councillor Miss Dorothy Trott

of the Committee for Education. During her year of office as Sheriff, the Canford Cliffs ward committee decided not to support her re-election to the council, on the ground of her age. Unperturbed, Miss Trott stood as an independent Conservative candidate, but was narrowly defeated by the official Conservative.

WHEATLEY, Lt.-Col. Sir Mervyn James, Freeman of Poole, Mayor of Poole 1936, former MP for East Dorset (1945-50) and for Poole (1950-51), Government Whip 1949-51, Deputy Lieutenant of Dorset 1952, KBE 1952, President of Poole Conservative Association 1953-1967, died in October 1974 at the age of 94. He served in the Dorset Regiment 1898-1918. He was one of the members of Dorset Volunteer Active Service Company who were admitted as Freemen in 1901 for their service in the Boer War. During the Second World War he commanded Poole Home Guard from 1940-1945.

WHITELOCK, Frederick George. Retired in 1969 after a 51-year association with Poole Grammar School, which he entered as a pupil and returned to as a newly qualified master. He founded the Science VI form in 1930 with one pupil, and saw it grow to more than 200. He was an outstanding teacher of his favourite subject, chemistry. From 1950 until his retirement he was deputy headmaster.

Mr F G Whitelock

POSTSCRIPT

Those members of the old Poole Borough Council who foresaw possible difficulties in meeting the final cost of the Arts Centre had shown surprisingly few misgivings when they earlier approved the spending of more than £7 million on the purchase from Lord Wimborne of some 530 acres of Canford Heath. They had been confident that both the capital and rolled-up interest would be more than recouped from sales of housing land when roads and services had been provided.

Shortly before Christmas 1975, members of the new District Council received notice from its Town Clerk and Chief Executive, Ian Andrews, of a meeting of the Council on January 6, 1976. It would discuss an interim report by the District Auditor, Mr A J Kappler, on the difficult situation it faced in financing capital expenditure.

Completion of the audits of the accounts of the old Borough Council for 1973 and 1974, as well as those of the present Council for the year ended March 31, 1975, was still delayed by a number of minor objections to them, primarily relating to open space. While these peevish and somewhat pedantic issues remained unresolved, the objector could have had no idea of their effect upon the timing of the sensation that would be caused by the District Auditor's interim report. Among other things, it would provide a platform for any member of the new council who wished to pass judgement upon certain actions of the old one.

The Policy and Resources Committee of the new Council had discussed the auditor's interim report at a meeting on December 16, but this was the first time that most members had seen a copy. Its main concern was that the value of the land in Stage II of the Canford Heath development had decreased, due to the financial constraints in the property market, caused by the Middle East oil crisis. Profits from land sales had been expected to provide substantial help in funding a number of capital projects. They included the Arts Centre, for which the current estimated cost had risen to more than £4 million.

The District Auditor's remit to report on local authority accounts had recently been extended. He was no longer confined to report merely on the legality and accuracy of accounts, but could also offer management advice. In the discharge of this new power, he warned of possible difficulties in funding the development at Canford Heath if the Council continued its policy of not selling land in depressed market conditions.

Expenditure of £5.2m (including capitalised interest of £1.28m) on the South Canford Heath site, which is mainly to provide land and services for private housing development, is at present financed by temporary borrowing, pending the proceeds of sale of the developed land.

The scheme is continuing, and the gross cost, including capitalised interest, may exceed £16m, he wrote. The auditor calculated what the position on funding Canford Heath, the Arts Centre, and other capital projects would be at the beginning of the 1977/78 financial year. He forecast *a balance which was expected to exceed £6m for which no borrowing powers will be available and which it is intended to finance by the sale of property owned by the authority. Completion of the sales necessary to produce the required sum and their timing in relation to the finance required is crucial, and any shortfall could result in a charge to the rate fund.*

The magnitude of the problem is indicated by comparing the sum to be financed, £6m, and the product of a penny rate which, in 1975/6, is expected to be £162,600. The Council should continue to call for up-to-date reports on the cost of each of these schemes and on the prospects for financing them so that informed decisions may be taken if rates of interest, property values or other circumstances change.

The situation, as portrayed by the District Auditor, came as a considerable shock to members of the council. Some critics readily ascribed it to 'gross mismanagement by a few, and the apathy of many others.' The report was leaked to the media well in advance of the Council meeting called for January 6. As soon as the Bournemouth *Evening Echo* revealed its substance, other local and national media avidly gave their own interpretations of it. Not to put too fine a point upon Mr Kappler's words, they suggested that the Council was now saddled with a £6 million debt as the result of an unsuccessful £16 million land speculation on Canford Heath. By dividing £6 million by £162,000, the current product of a 1p rate, it was also possible to engender fears of a massive rate rise in 1977-78. The District Auditor's statement that the Council proposed to fund the £6m from sales of assets was much less astonishing, and largely overlooked.

Arthur Lloyd-Allen had been chairman of the Finance Committee of the old Council when the Canford Heath development began. He was now chairman of the Policy and Resources Committee of the new Council. Its members looked to him for reassurance and a rebuttal of the more outrageous rumours that the town was, in effect, bankrupt, and would not be able to go on paying its contractors and investors.

On January 6, 1976, he sought the indulgence of the Council to make a speech longer than that permitted by standing orders. He promised there would be no substantial increase in rates for the following year; that there was no threat to the security of investors, who would continue to receive payments of interest and capital on the due dates; and that contractors and suppliers would continue to be paid.

It was not the first time Poole Council had faced such problems. He had been told by the District Auditor that there was no criticism of any of its decisions to go ahead with the capital schemes in question. 'We have set out to achieve a lot more than many similar sized authorities,' he admitted, 'and in doing so we have not made life easy for ourselves or our officers.'

Councillor Lloyd-Allen had no quarrel with the District Auditor's warning that the timing of sales of Council assets would be crucial, and that any shortfall could result in a charge to the rate fund. He said the assets to be disposed of had already been identified. Many of them were in the form of industrial land, which unlike housing land had kept its value and was still keenly sought. The Council was not having to dispose of all its assets. Its balance sheet showed a £7m surplus of assets, at their original cost, over liabilities. At current valuations, the Council could realise assets worth £77 million against loan debts totalling £23 million. 'We have been dealing, as any Council does, for years in land for redevelopment and development purposes, and will continue to do so.'

Turning to media reports which implied that £6m in cash would have to be found by the following April, he affirmed that the Council would at no time have to raise £6m. He was also confident that there would be no extraordinary pressure on it in fixing next year's rate. The only burden on the rates would arise if the Council was unable to extend the period for deferring interest charges on the Canford Heath development. As for its £16m gross cost, to which the auditor had referred, the development was a long-term project of at least ten years. To arrive at this sum, it was necessary to take the present situation, where the Corporation had provided a water supply, roads and sewers, for land which it had not sold; capitalise the cost and interest; and then extrapolate these costs over the probable term of the development.

He ended prophetically by saying: 'I am sure my statement will not satisfy those who - by nature, it seems - set out to criticise Poole Council or any of its activities.'

It did not satisfy the national media. The *Daily Mail* report on January 7 was headed *Council backs £16m loser.* In *The Times* it was claimed that the District Auditor had criticised 'a development scheme involving speculative land purchases.' Its report was headed *No action by council after £6m debt warning by auditor,* and quoted Councillor Mrs Adams as saying: 'The fault is that our amateur speculators tangled themselves up in these huge land purchases long after the wide boys had ceased to buy.'

Southern Television carried an inflammatory report, claiming the Council was '£6m in the red,' caused by 'a property speculation...in the hope of a quick fortune.' It asserted that the project was undertaken to finance 'prestige town centre amenities,' and that 'if the down-turn in the property market continues for any length of time, ratepayers will be faced ultimately with additional huge sums.' Finally it maintained that provision of new civic amenities would be 'fairly restricted' over the next five years.

The *Daily Mail* returned to the fray in its issue of January 14, 1976. It referred to 'a damning report from the District Auditor about their financial difficulties,' which had been presented to councillors. It said the public gallery was packed with local residents who looked in open-mouthed bewilderment as speaker after speaker claimed *there was no problem,* and one member *even suggested that they should pass a vote of thanks to the officers who, many years ago, had first suggested the scheme.* The writer said that if the government refused a request to waive interest charges [a proposal which had never been contemplated] *and left Poole to get into the kind of financial mess that would mean bankruptcy for any private firm... the message would sink in.*

The District Auditor was asked by Poole's Chief Executive to comment on the statement in the *Daily Mail* that he [Mr Kappler] had warned the Council that *they simply would not be able to afford to pay the interest, let alone the capital, on loans they had raised for a blatant piece of land speculation.* He replied: 'My report will show that I certainly did not say that the Council would not be able to afford to pay the interest on loans they had raised, and I did not refer to the matter as a blatant piece of land speculation - indeed, such a stricture would have been most unfair.'

However severe the storm, the clouds eventually clear. It was true that for the year 1976/77 the rate fund had to contribute to the costs of Canford Heath's loan charges, but it was much less than the equivalent of a 1p rate. The following year, the District Auditor reported: *The economic selling price of the remaining land will be over £50,000 per acre, which is well above the present market price, although it has increased over the last two years.* Time was still testing the truth of Councillor Lloyd-Allen's assertion in January 1976 that the difficulties were ones 'which by continued industry and goodwill we will overcome without any shortfall.'

The first development on Canford Heath took ten years to complete and yielded a surplus of more than £600,000 to the Council. The position in later years of the second one is best summarised in the Borough Treasurer's annual financial review at the end of 1989. Expenditure on the project had totalled £19.09 million, of which £8.07m was for land and £6.76m for net interest. Income from land sales totalled £28.38m, and produced a contribution to the cost of the Ashdown sports centre of £1.2m. The current surplus on the scheme was just under £10.5m. Approximately 324 acres had been sold at an average price of £87,617 an acre. One sale of 1.2 acres to a housing association in the current year had been at a price equivalent to £525,000 an acre. A further 33.41 acres of land could potentially be developed, to yield an estimated £15m. Half of this area, however, was the subject of sensitive environmental issues, which might reduce the sales revenue from £15m to £6m.

INDEX OF SUBJECTS

Hants and Dorset Motor Services, 68,
  183
Hants and Dorset Mineral Water, 24
harbour, 131, 175
Harbour Commissioners, 93, 99, 113,
  131, 133, 187
Hardy, Thomas, 111, 112
Hart, Ronald, 20, 21, 56, 109, 123, 124,
  143, 163
Haskins, Wilfred, 122, 143, 146
Hatch Pond Road, 74, 75
Hawker, Robert, 133
Haymoor Road, 127
Haynes, A B, 77
Health Committee, 89, 125
Health Visitors, 86
Heath, Edward, 127, 137
Herbert Avenue, 139
Herbert Carter School, 139
Hewitt, Rhodam, 179
Hickinson. Elsie, 42, 114, 118, 185
High Street, 9, 13, 15, 17, 24, 29, 34, 47,
  105, 114, 143
Hill Street, 28, 29, 71
Hillier, Parker, May & Rowden, 31
Hills, Don, 120
Holes Bay, 14, 75, 106
Home Help Service, 86
Honorary Aldermen, 122
Hopkins, Antony, 155
Hopkinson, Geoffrey, 25, 31, 83, 120,
  157
Horn, Captain C H, 133
Hospital Management Committee, 58
  hotels, 29, 87, 102, 152
Housing
  Council estates, 59
  elderly persons, 58, 59
  habitable standards, 88
  improvement areas, 89
  key workers' scheme, 57
  private ownership, 60, 63
  standard amenities, 89

Housing Act, 1969, 89
Housing and Local Government,
  Minister of, 175
  Ministry of, 25, 61
Housing Committee, 162, 179
Housing Manager, 57, 58
Hunger Hill, 14, 15, 28, 72, 75
Hussein, King, 161
Hutchinson, Alan, 154, 186
Hutton, Dr James, 179

I Industrial Training Unit, 105
industry, 57, 76, 101, 102, 121, 127
Inskip Housing Association, 58

J Jolliffe House, 14
Junior Accident Prevention Council,
  70

K King Street, 24, 28, 78
Kingland Road, 31, 34, 35, 37,
  110, 154, 155, 157, 158, 172
Knapp, William, 112

L Labour Party, 49, 78, 123, 124
Ladies' Walking Field, 35, 37, 39
Lagland Street, 11, 13, 25, 28, 99,
  139
Land and Natural Resources,
  Minister of, 133
Land Securities, 33
le Carré, John, 186
Lennon, John, 186
Libraries Committee, 42, 114, 154
  library service, 139, 140, 142
  mobile library, 139
Lilliput, 67
Links Road, 73
Lloyd-Allen, Arthur, 39, 40, 43, 62, 89,
  114, 118, 120, 122, 123, 128, 142,
  143, 156, 157, 158, 179, 186, 192,
  194
Local Government Act, 1958, 175

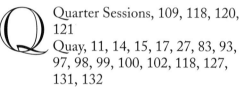

Roberts, Geoffrey, 78, 179
Rockley Sands, 29, 127, 143, 145, 152
Rockley, Lord, 188
Rogers, Graham, 180
Rogers' Almshouses, 28
Roman Catholic Church, 14
Rowe, Fred, 29, 55, 56, 75, 102, 110, 113,
    115, 117, 123, 143, 144, 146, 149,
    162, 179, 188, 189
Royal Commission on Local
    Government, 176
Royal Institute of Chartered Surveyors,
    152
Royal Marines, 115, 116, 117, 118, 131,
    133, 134, 137, 162
        Sir Ian Gourlay, CGRM, 118
        Special Boat Section, 116, 117
Royal Motor Yacht Club, 120, 137
Royal National Lifeboat Institution, 105,
    128
Royal Ordnance Factory, 102
Royal visits, 77, 89, 90, 142

S Sainsbury's, 42
Salvation Army, 28
Sandbanks, 67, 71, 100, 113, 118,
    133, 134, 138, 152, 153, 168, 183,
186
Sandbanks Road, 118, 152
Scaplen's Court, 114, 115
Scrase, Leslie, 179
Seldown Lane, 154
Serpentine Lane, 15, 16, 35, 47
Serpentine Road, 47, 48, 49, 51
Sewage, 66, 67, 68, 128
    diversion, 66
    purification works, 67
Sharp, Dame Evelyn, 61
Shaw, Leonard, 42
Sherrin, Tom, 111, 152, 188
Shore Road, 67, 171
Short, Bernard, 188
Sieger, Joshua, 105, 115, 188

Silver, George, 168, 189
Simmonds, William, 122
Sir Peter Thompson's House, 11, 14
Sidney, Ann, 111
Slums, 9, 21, 128
Social activities, 109, 116, 160
Society of Poole Men, 112
South East Dorset and South West
    Hampshire Study, 64
South Road, 25, 82, 139, 140, 142, 154
South-East Study, 175
Southern Gas Board, 83, 98, 99, 172
Southern Ocean Shipyard, 137
Southern Television, 56, 83, 155, 193
South-Western Pottery, 102
Speed limit, 73
Sport, Minister of, 146
Sports Centre, 43, 64, 125, 143, 146
Squatters, 19
St James' Parish Church, 109, 112, 114
St Mary's Roman Catholic Church, 105
Stadium, 48, 105, 127
Steptoe, James, 84, 115, 156, 157, 189
Sterte, 9, 13, 15
Stokes, Bert, 189
Strike, dustmen, 76
Styring, Frederick, 14
Sunday Times, 35
Swan Lake Cafe, 168
Swanage, 70
Swimming bath, 171
    indoor, 172
    open air, 172

T Telephone exchanges, 126
Templeman, Philip, 90
Thames Street, 17, 21, 114
The Times, 16, 35, 83, 193
Thompson, A A, 145
Torrey Canyon, 132
Tourism, 152
    official guide, 153
    tourist attractions –

INDEX OF ILLUSTRATIONS

and top windows are
34 first floor windows
filled in except
right front

36

38

40   42

36

4 brick fin

Market Street

painted brick facade
dark colour used for plinth

render finish

render finish   Brick finish .SITE
                            O.F.
                          GUILDHALL

1.
This sketch shows the important part played
by a conservative use of wall finish materials.
warm dark bricks and cream coloured renders are
dominant in the street, creating unity, but providing
a supplementary interest in the reflection of light
and shade in scene.

perfectly with the cream coloured render and warm
dark brickwork of its setting. The beauty of the extern
stairway is definitely understated.
This building paid for by the town's two M.P.'s of the pe
reflects admirably the civic pride of a small seaport
town at a time of prosperity. In its modest way it is
unimpossible in its setting as the great buildings of
a capital city. To a great extent it conveys a
personal warmth and charm.

Market Street

The G

JOHN

This sketch portrays a true scale and character of much of ov
twisting streets enclosed mainly by neat humble dwellings in the ov
Alterations to some of the buildings have revealed cores of much earlier